Maps for U.S. History
Map Resource Book

Artists: Pat St. Onge and Bill Beard
Editor: Mary Dieterich
Proofreaders: Margaret Brown and Alexis Fey

COPYRIGHT © 2024 Mark Twain Media, Inc.

ISBN 978-1-62223-890-3

Printing No. CD-405083

Mark Twain Media, Inc., Publishers
Distributed by Carson-Dellosa Publishing LLC

The purchase of this book entitles the buyer to reproduce the student pages for classroom use only. Other permissions may be obtained by writing Mark Twain Media, Inc., Publishers.

All rights reserved. Printed in the United States of America.

Visit us at www.marktwainpublishing.com

Table of Contents

Introduction iv

#	Title	Page
001	Migration Patterns of Early Americans	1
002	Native American Culture Groups With Tribe Names	2
003	Voyages of Eric the Red and Leif Ericson	3
004	The Four Voyages of Columbus	4
005	The Columbian Exchange	5
006	Spanish Exploration in the New World	6
007	Voyages of Discovery	7
008	Early Explorers of North America With Modern State Borders	8
009	Expedition of Francisco Vasquez de Coronado, 1540–1542 With State Borders & Labels	9
010	Major Native American Tribes in the 1600s	10
011	First British Settlements in America	11
012	Slave Trade From Africa to the Americas, 1650 to 1860	12
013	The Triangular Trade	13
014	The Thirteen British Colonies in America	14
015	The New England Colonies	15
016	The Middle Colonies	16
017	The Southern Colonies	17
018	Economics of the British Colonies	18
019	French, Spanish, and English Land Claims Prior to the French and Indian War	19
020	Land Taken From Native Americans, Before 1750–1810	20
021	The French and Indian War, 1754–1763: French and British Forts	21
022	Territorial Claims in the French and Indian War, 1754–1763 With Troop Movements and Battle Victories	22
023	The Proclamation Line of 1763	23
024	Treaty of Paris, 1763	24
025	Midnight Rides of Paul Revere, William Dawes, and Samuel Prescott: All Routes	25
026	Battles of Lexington and Concord, April 18–19, 1775	26
027	Battles of the American Revolution	27
028	Treaty of Paris, 1783	28
029	Territorial Acquisitions, 1783–1853	29
030	Northwest Territory, 1787	30
031	Early Roads to the West	31
032	Louisiana Purchase, 1803	32
033	Lewis and Clark Expedition, 1804–1806	33
034	War of 1812 With Troop Movements	34
035	Westward Expansion, 1815–1845	35
036	Acquisition of Florida, 1819	36
037	Missouri Compromise, 1820	37
038	Removal of Native Americans, 1820–1840	38
039	Trail of Tears and the Cherokee Removal, 1830s	39
040	Western Trails	40
041	The Santa Fe Trail	41
042	The Oregon Trail	42
043	The Mormon Trail	43
044	Important Canals, 1840	44
045	Texas War for Independence With Troop Movements and Battles	45
046	Northwest Boundary Established	46
047	Oregon Country	47

Table of Contents (Cont.)

048	The War with Mexico, 1846–1848: Famous Battles With Troop Movements	48
049	Major Gold Strikes in the California Gold Rush, 1848–1859	49
050	Compromise of 1850	50
051	Kansas-Nebraska Act, 1854	51
052	Bleeding Kansas, 1854–1858	52
053	United States in 1856: Free States, Slave States, and Territories	53
054	Pony Express Route	54
055	The Underground Railroad	55
056	Resources of the Northern and Southern States Before 1860	56
057	Population Density of Enslaved Persons, 1860	57
058	Election of 1860	58
059	Railroads Prior to the Civil War	59
060	Union and Confederate States	60
061	Civil War Strategy	61
062	Early Battles of the Civil War, 1861–1862	62
063	Civil War Battles, 1862–1863	63
064	Battle of Gettysburg	64
065	Final Civil War Battles, 1864–1865	65
066	Reconstruction: Dates of Readmission to the Union and Reestablished Conservative Governments	66
067	Major Battles With Native Americans, 1860–1890	67
068	The Chisholm and Other Cattle Trails of the Western United States	68
069	States and Territories of the United States, 1868–1876	69
070	Transcontinental Railroad	70
071	Railroads and Growth in the West, 1890	71
072	Immigration, 1870–1900	72
073	Routes of the Klondike Gold Rush	73
074	Spanish-American War	74
075	Dust Bowl, 1930s	75
076	Climate Regions of the United States	76

Introduction

Maps for U.S. History provides teachers, parents, and students with a selection of high-quality maps for classroom and homeschool use. From the first exploration and settlement of the Americas to the post-Civil War years, these maps will complement your social studies curriculum as you study the history of the United States.

These black and white maps are all reproducible for student use. They can also be made into transparencies or scanned into digital files for use with a classroom projection device. The ebook version includes some color maps, and the digital files are ready for printing or projection.

This collection of maps provides handy resources for illustrating the geography of historical events, such as settlement, wars, trade, peace agreements, and territorial expansion. Students will be able to practice their geography skills by using the map keys to decipher symbols, discovering the landforms represented on the maps, and gauging distances using the map scales. Many of the maps are related, showing changes over time. Use the maps with your own curriculum in a variety of ways to reinforce the five themes of geography: location, place, region, movement, and human-environment interaction.

Photo credit: US Navy 090707-N-4031K-001 Amy Gardner, wife of Naval Air Facility Atsugi Commanding Officer Capt. Eric Gardner, tutors Japanese students on geography at the base food court.jpg {PD-USNavy} 7 Jul. 2009. Mass Communication Specialist 2nd Class Steven Khor. <https://commons.wikimedia.org/wiki/File:US_Navy_090707-N-4031K-001_Amy_Gardner,_wife_of_Naval_Air_Facility_Atsugi_Commanding_Officer_Capt._Eric_Gardner,_tutors_Japanese_students_on_geography_at_the_base_food_court.jpg>

Name: _____ Date: _____

Migration Patterns of Early Americans

Maps for U.S. History | Migration Patterns of Early Americans

Map #: 001

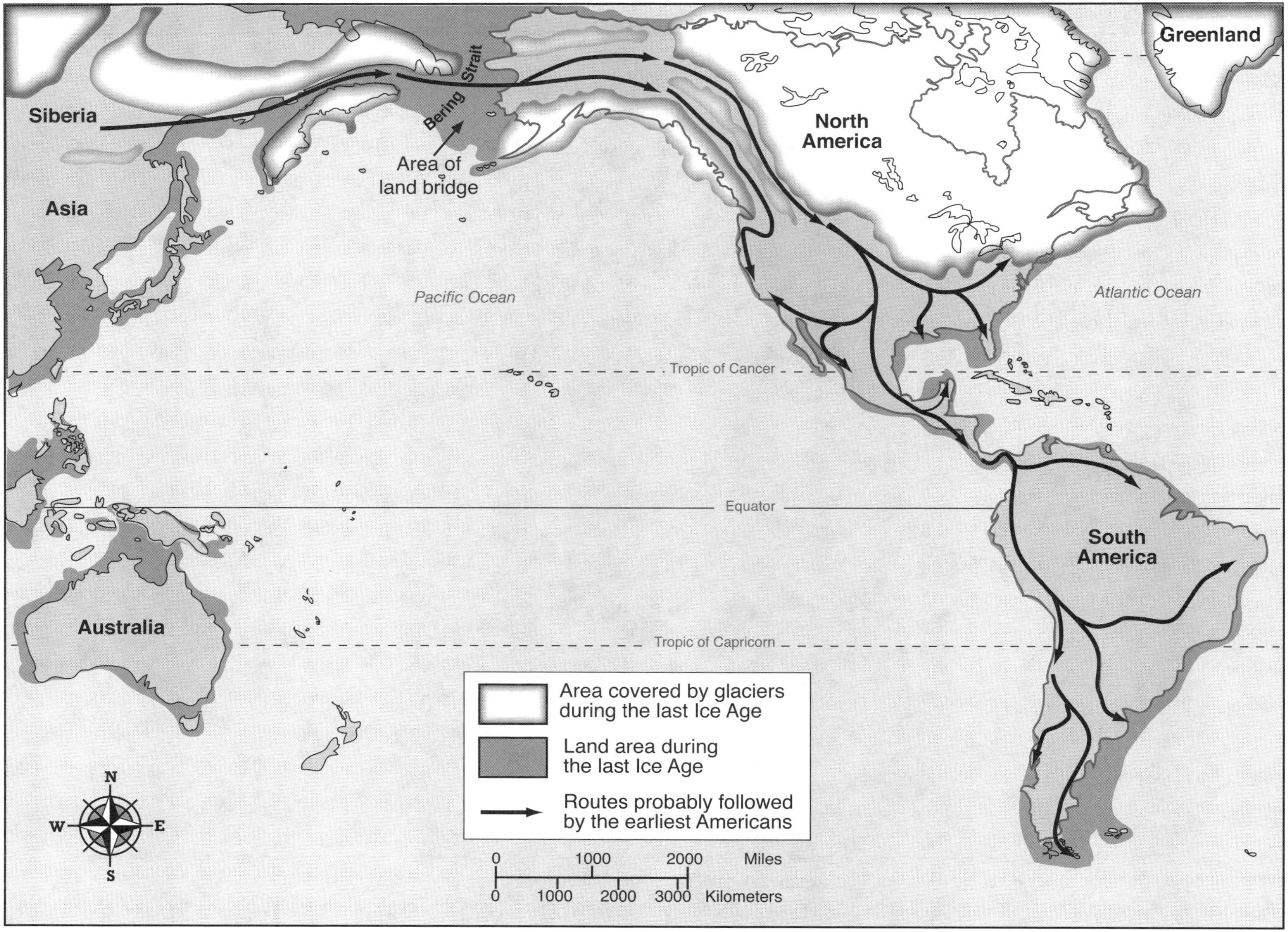

Legend:
- Area covered by glaciers during the last Ice Age
- Land area during the last Ice Age
- Routes probably followed by the earliest Americans

Labels on map: Greenland, North America, South America, Atlantic Ocean, Pacific Ocean, Australia, Asia, Siberia, Bering Strait, Area of land bridge, Tropic of Cancer, Equator, Tropic of Capricorn

Scale: 0–3000 Kilometers / 0–2000 Miles

CD-405083 ©Mark Twain Media, Inc., Publishers

Name: _____ Date: _____

Native American Culture Groups With Tribe Names

Maps for U.S. History — Native American Culture Groups With Tribe Names

Map #: 002

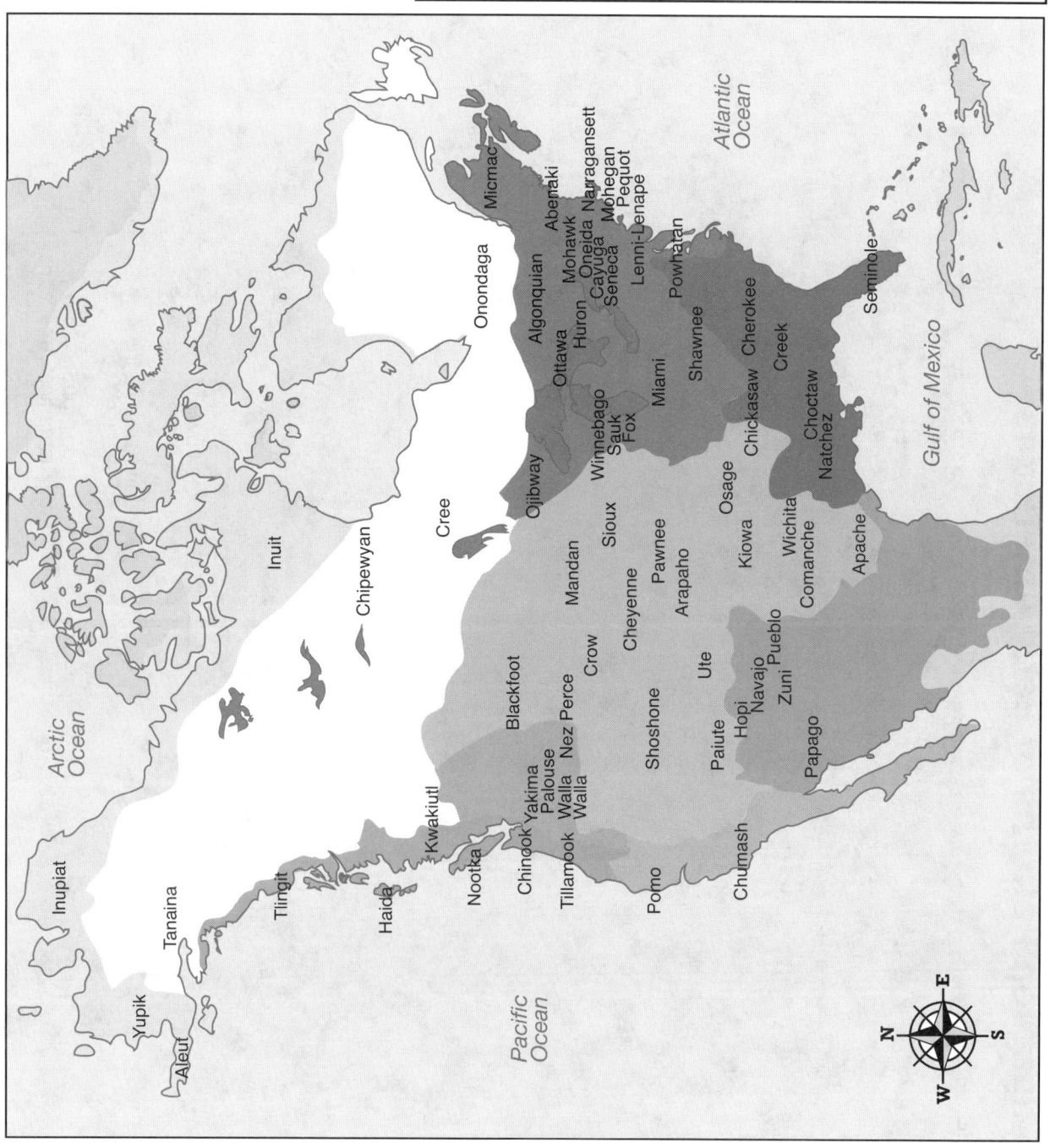

Culture Groups
- Arctic
- California
- Great Basin
- Northeast
- Northwest Coast
- Great Plains
- Plateau
- Southeast
- Southwest
- Subarctic

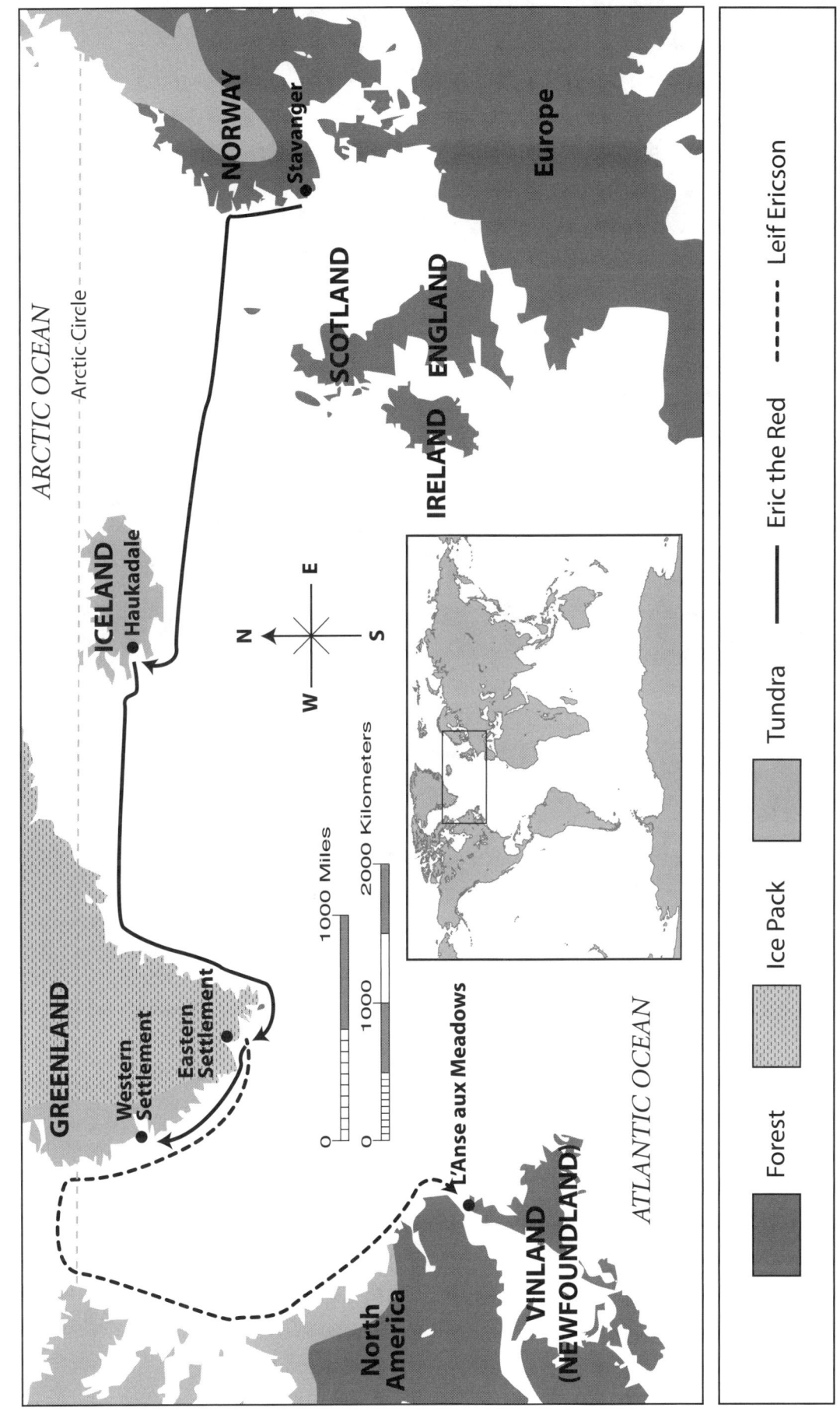

Name: _____ Date: _____

The Four Voyages of Columbus

Maps for U.S. History · The Four Voyages of Columbus

Map #: 004

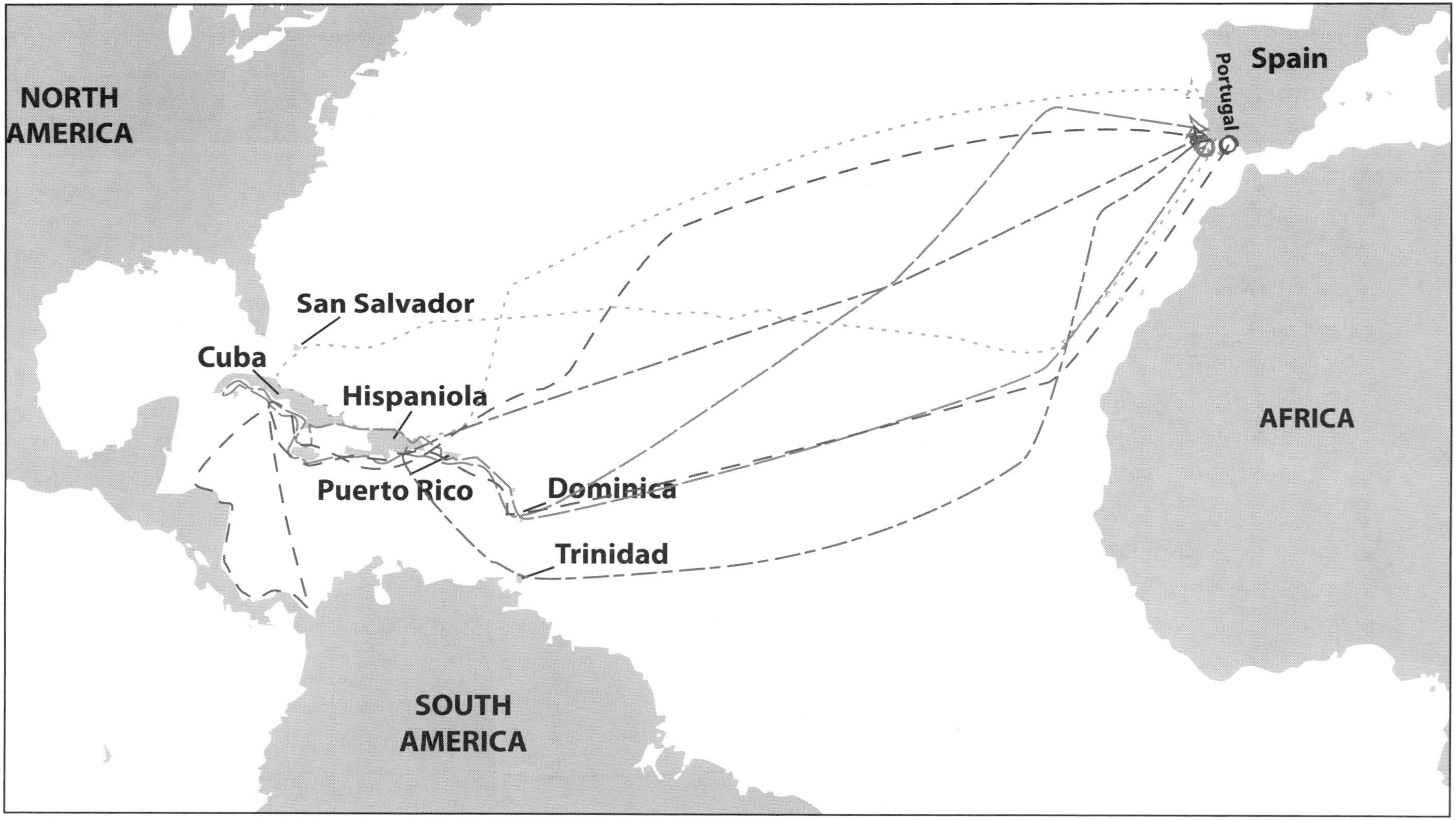

- .... First Voyage (1492–1493)
- ——— Second Voyage (1493–1496)
- —·—·— Third Voyage (1498–1500)
- — — — Fourth Voyage (1502–1504)

Locations labeled: Spain, Portugal, AFRICA, NORTH AMERICA, SOUTH AMERICA, San Salvador, Cuba, Hispaniola, Puerto Rico, Dominica, Trinidad

CD-405083 ©Mark Twain Media, Inc., Publishers

Name: _____ Date: _____

The Columbian Exchange

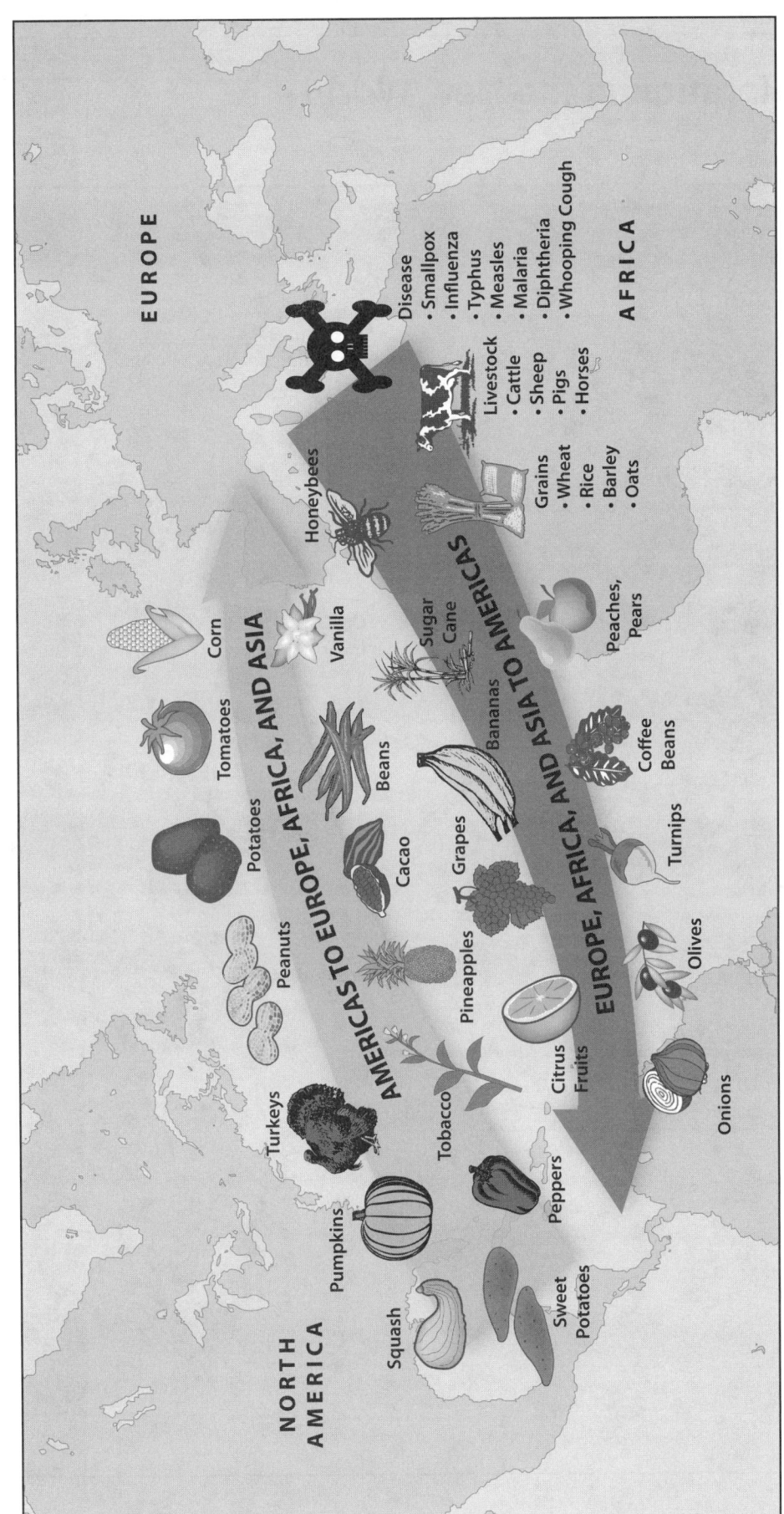

Maps for U.S. History | Spanish Exploration in the New World

Name: _____ Date: _____

Spanish Exploration in the New World

Map #: 006

Voyages of Discovery

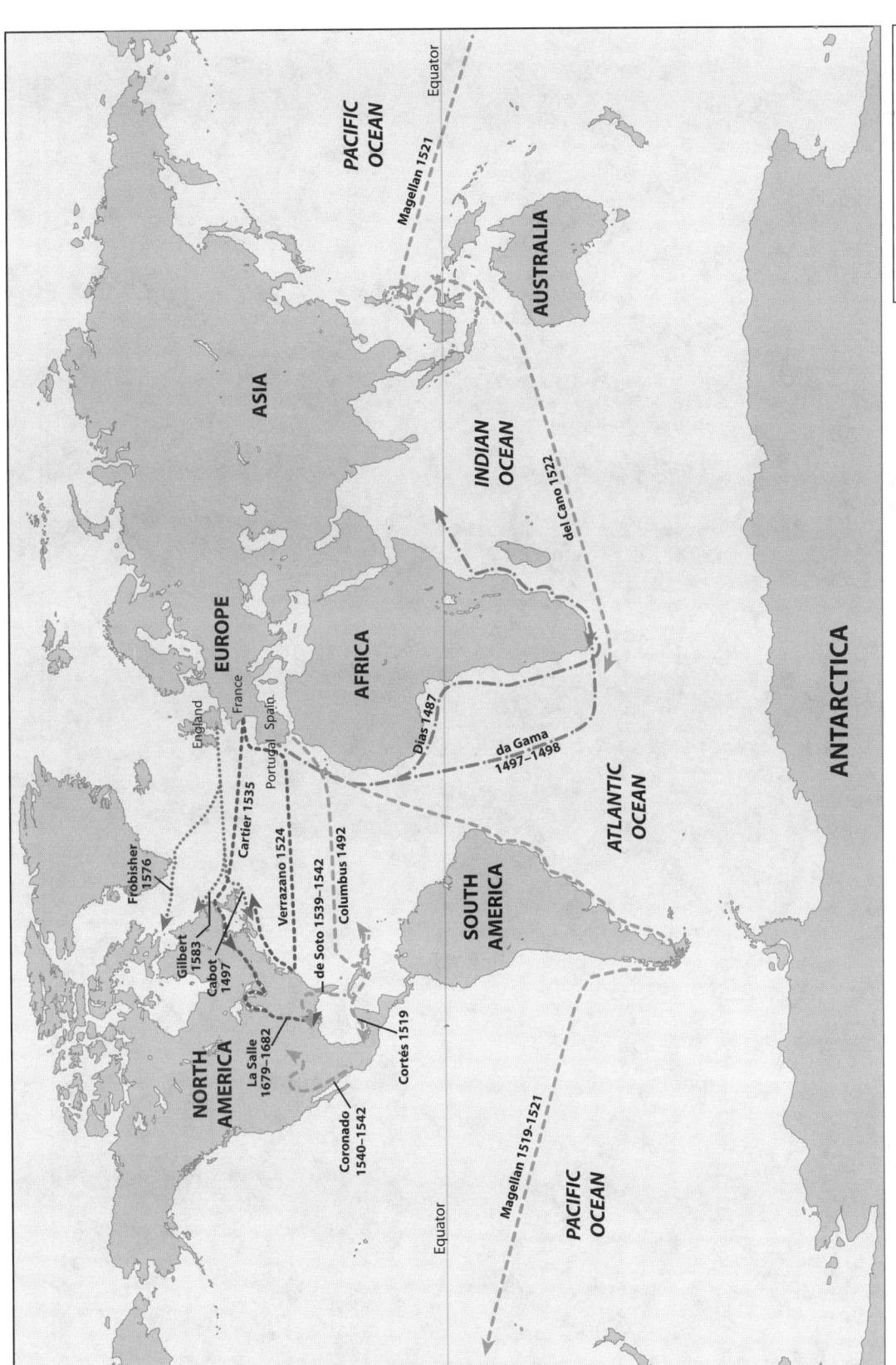

Name: _____ Date: _____

Early Explorers of North America With Modern State Borders

Maps for U.S. History — Early Explorers of North America With Modern State Borders

Map #: 008

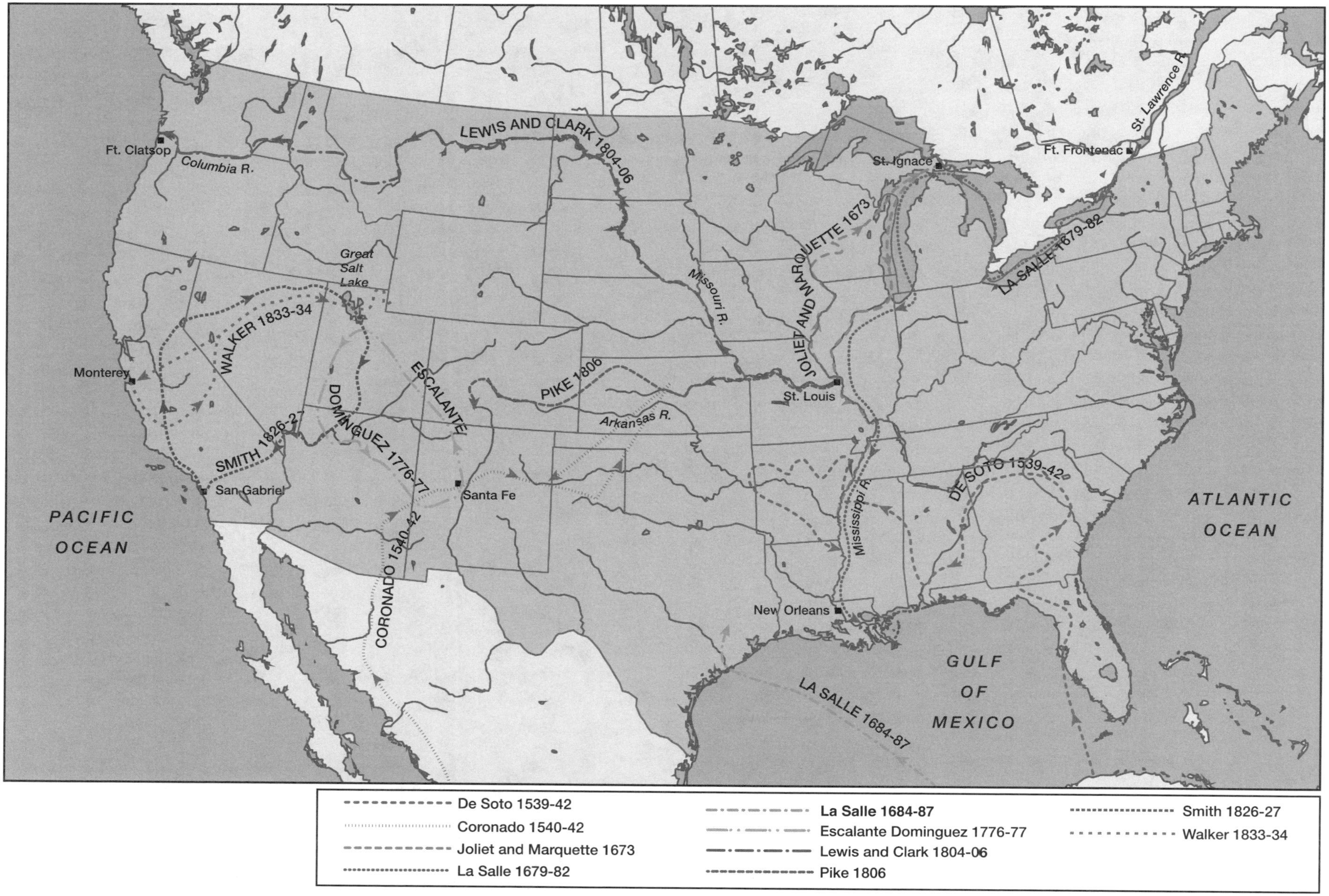

Legend:
- De Soto 1539–42
- Coronado 1540–42
- Joliet and Marquette 1673
- La Salle 1679–82
- La Salle 1684–87
- Escalante Dominguez 1776–77
- Lewis and Clark 1804–06
- Pike 1806
- Smith 1826–27
- Walker 1833–34

Labeled features: St. Lawrence R., Ft. Frontenac, St. Ignace, LA SALLE 1679–82, JOLIET AND MARQUETTE 1673, Mississippi R., DE SOTO 1539–42, New Orleans, LA SALLE 1684–87, Gulf of Mexico, Atlantic Ocean, St. Louis, Missouri R., Arkansas R., PIKE 1806, Santa Fe, CORONADO 1540–42, ESCALANTE DOMINGUEZ 1776–77, Great Salt Lake, LEWIS AND CLARK 1804–06, Columbia R., Ft. Clatsop, WALKER 1833–34, SMITH 1826–27, San Gabriel, Monterey, Pacific Ocean

Name: _____ Date: _____

Expedition of Francisco Vasquez de Coronado, 1540–1542 With State Borders and Labels

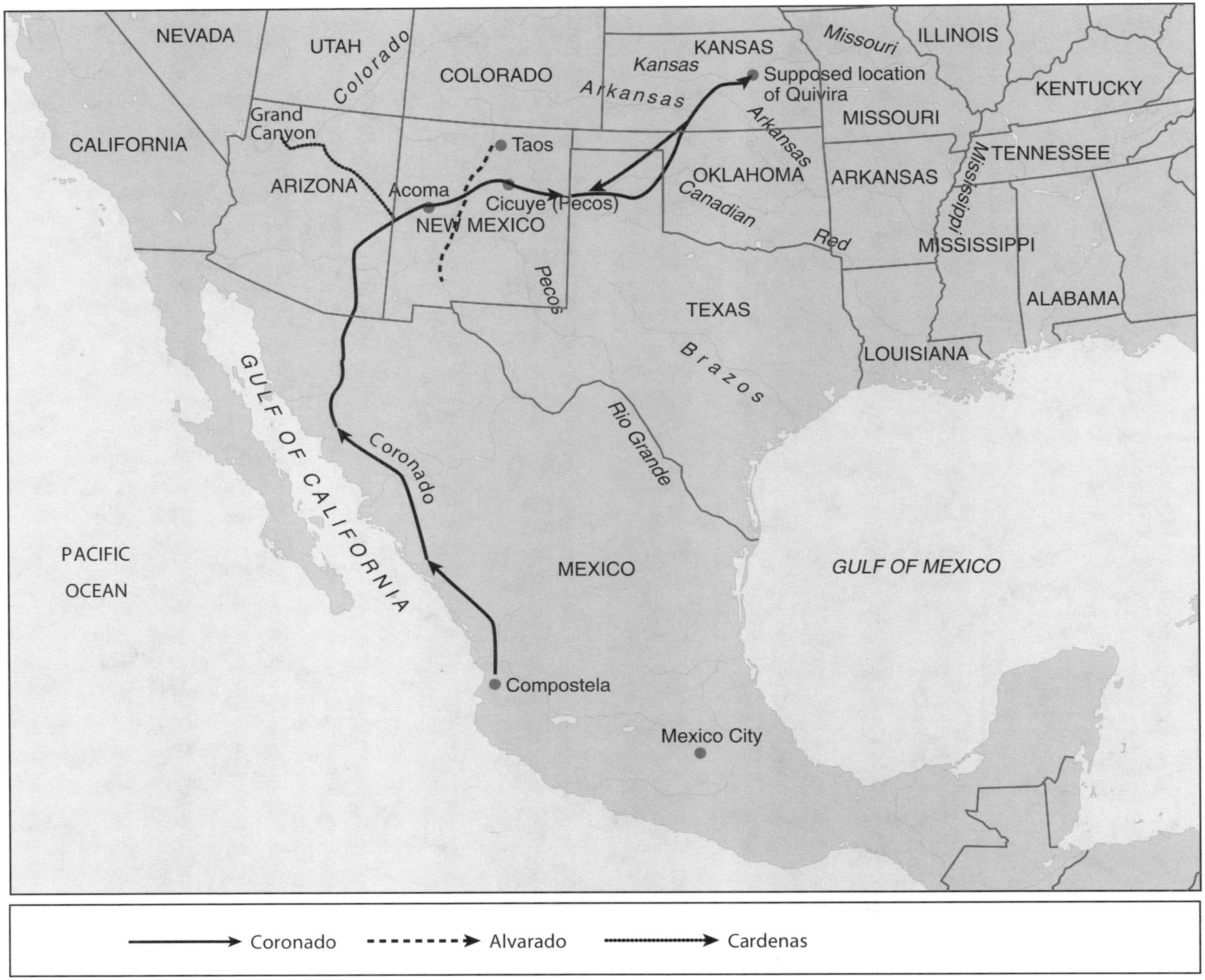

Maps for U.S. History

Major Native American Tribes in the 1600s

Name: _____ Date: _____

Major Native American Tribes in the 1600s

Map #: 010

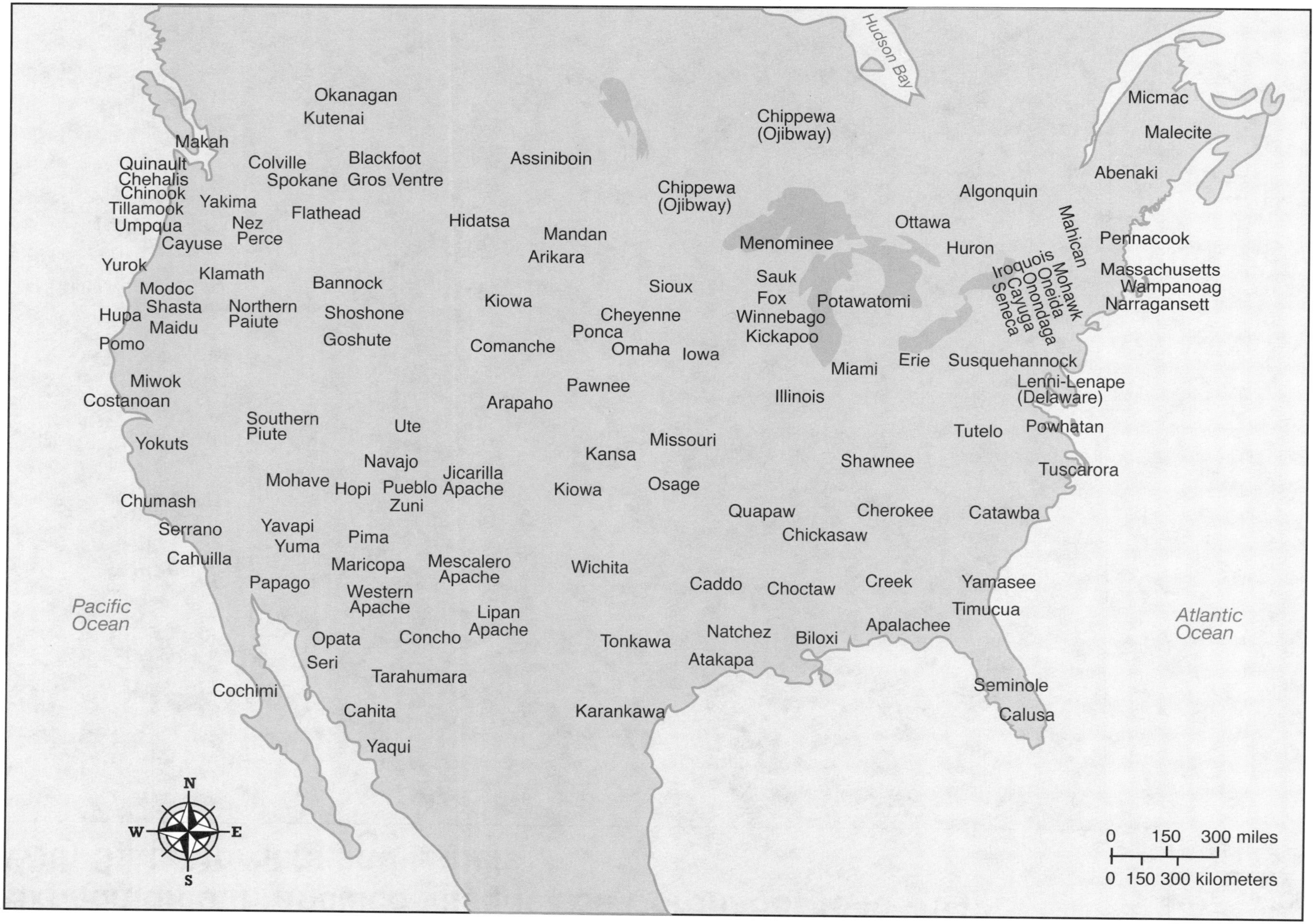

Maps for U.S. History

First British Settlements in America

Name: _____ Date: _____

First British Settlements in America

Map #: 011

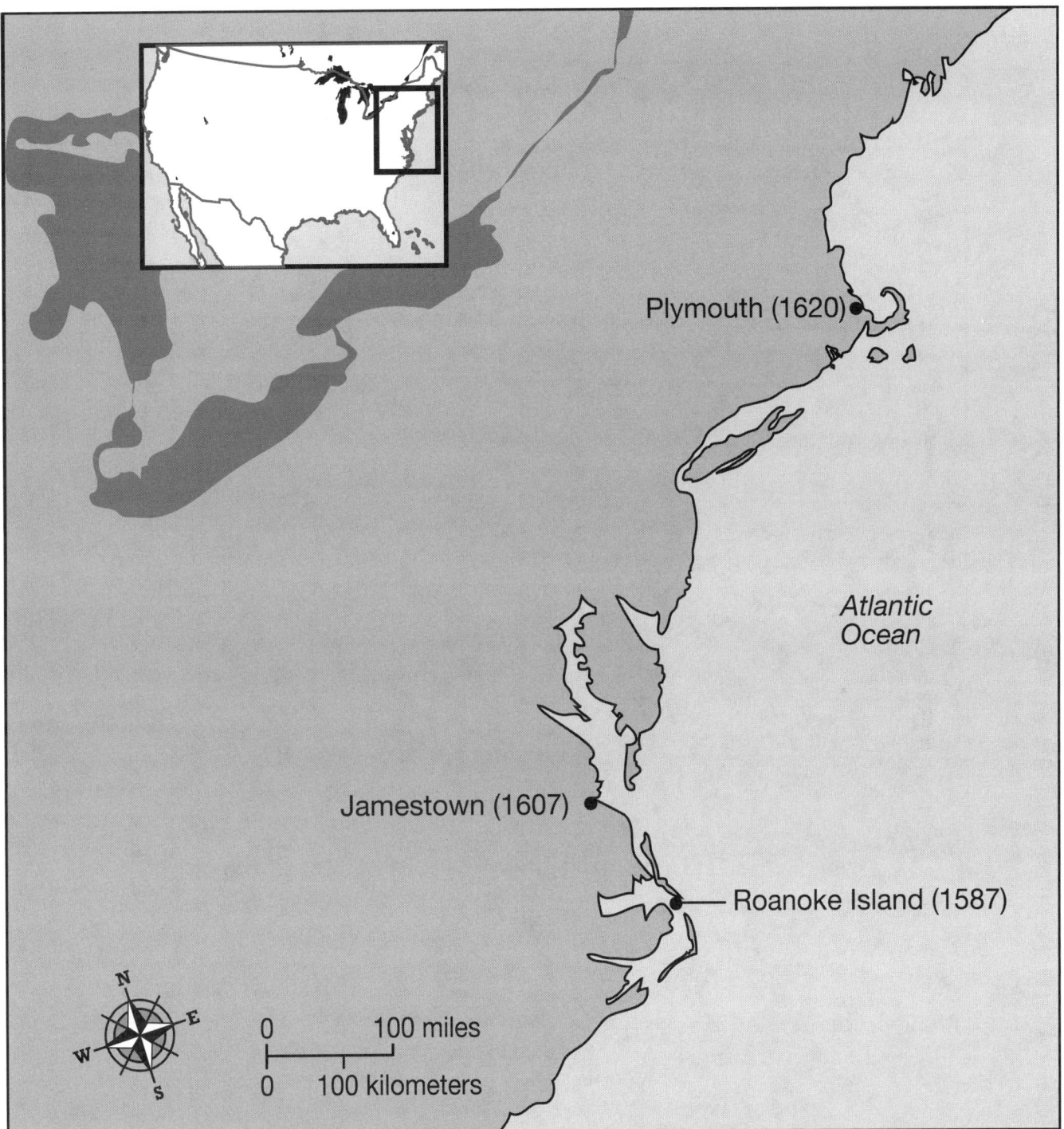

Slave Trade From Africa to the Americas, 1650 to 1860

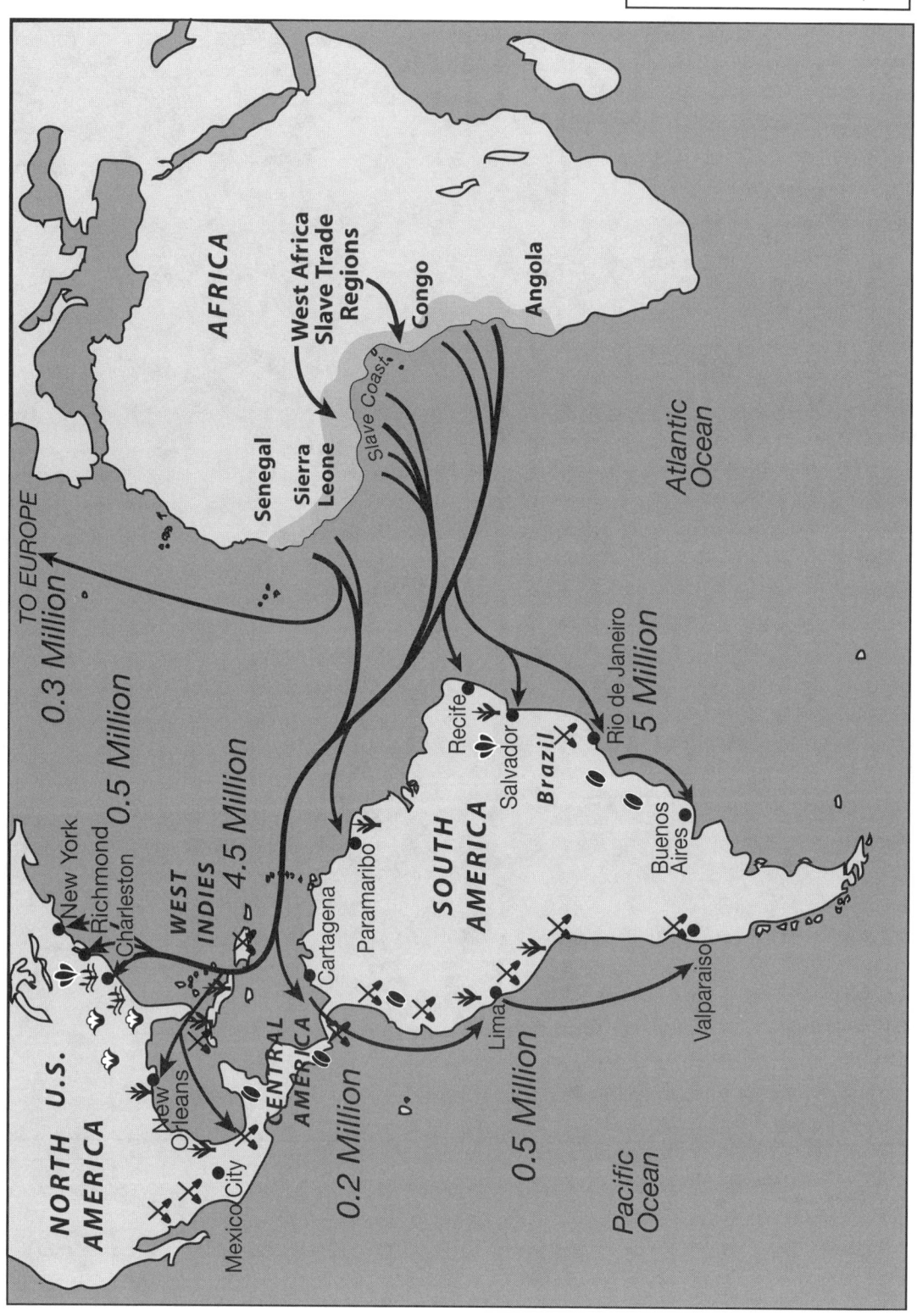

Name: _____ Date: _____

The Triangular Trade

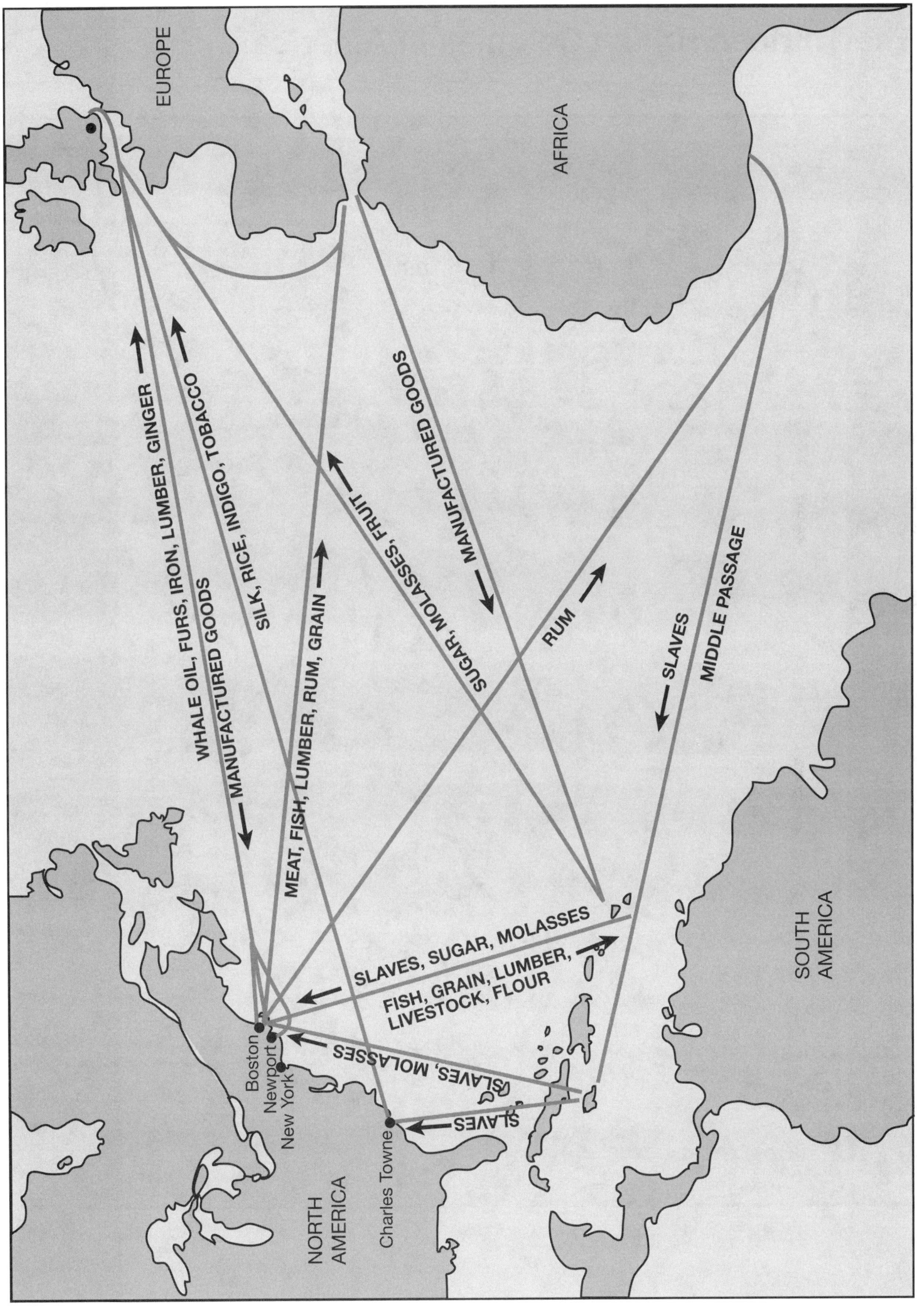

Maps for U.S. History

Map #: 013

The Triangular Trade

Labels on map:
- EUROPE
- AFRICA
- NORTH AMERICA
- SOUTH AMERICA
- Boston
- Newport
- New York
- Charles Towne

Trade routes:
- WHALE OIL, FURS, IRON, LUMBER, GINGER →
- MANUFACTURED GOODS ↓
- SILK, RICE, INDIGO, TOBACCO →
- MEAT, FISH, LUMBER, RUM, GRAIN →
- SUGAR, MOLASSES, FRUIT →
- MANUFACTURED GOODS ↓
- RUM →
- SLAVES ↓
- MIDDLE PASSAGE
- SLAVES, SUGAR, MOLASSES ←
- FISH, GRAIN, LUMBER, LIVESTOCK, FLOUR →
- SLAVES, MOLASSES ←
- SLAVES ←

CD-405083 ©Mark Twain Media, Inc., Publishers

Maps for U.S. History
The Thirteen British Colonies in America

Name: _____ Date: _____

The Thirteen British Colonies in America

Map #: 014

Maps for U.S. History

The New England Colonies

Name: _____ Date: _____

The New England Colonies

Map #: 015

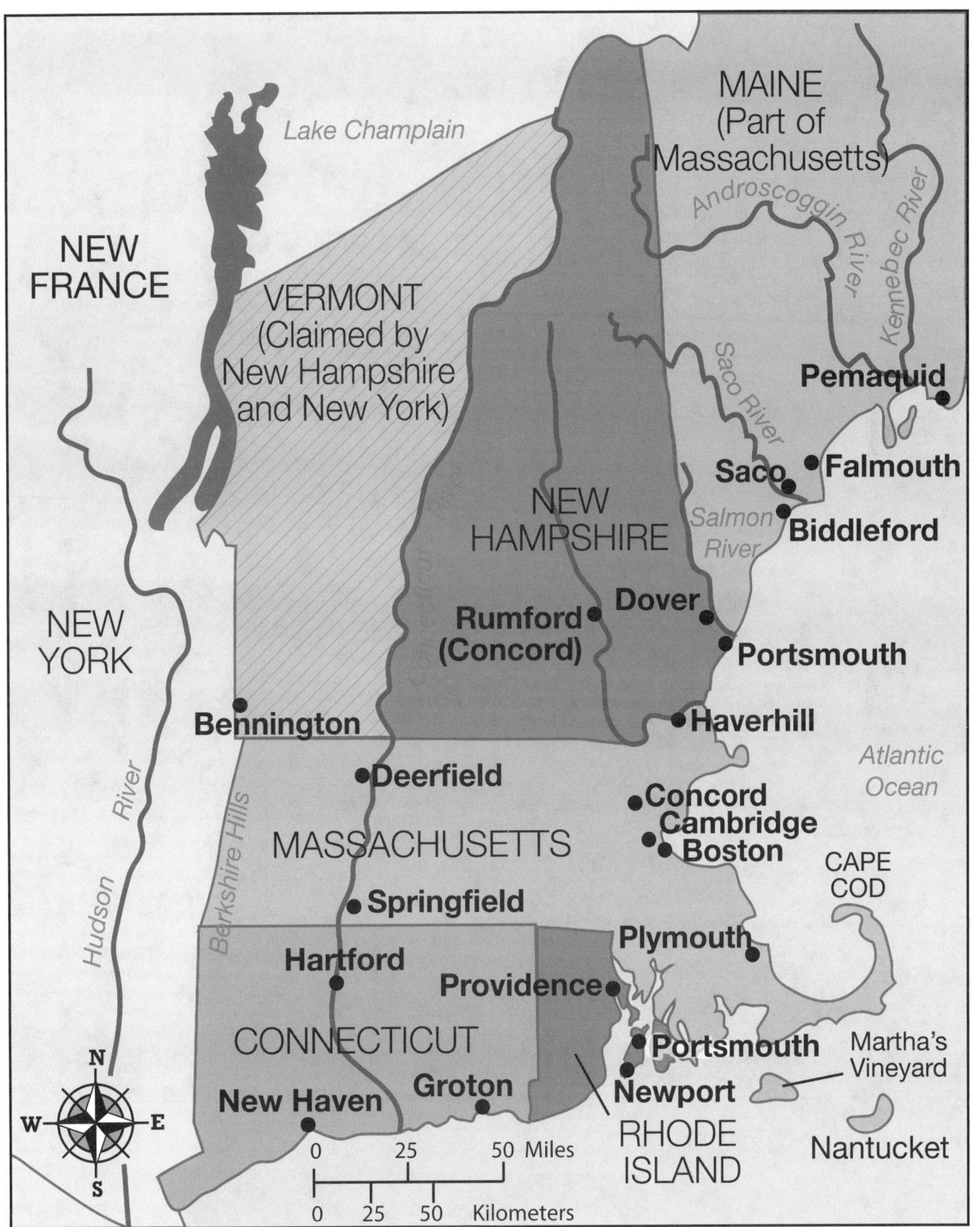

Maps for U.S. History The Middle Colonies

Name: _____ Date: _____

The Middle Colonies

Map #: 016

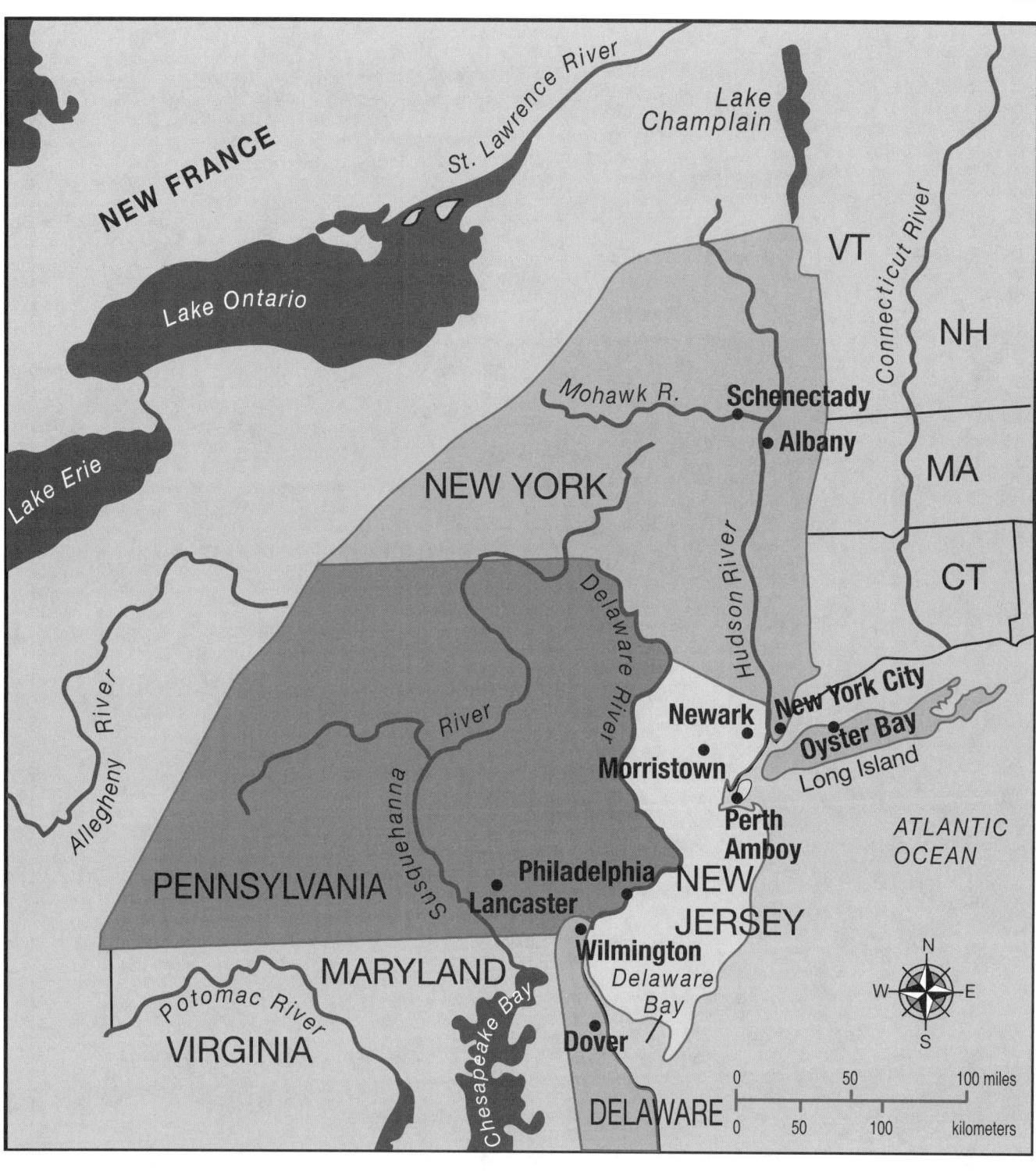

Maps for U.S. History

The Southern Colonies

Name: _____ Date: _____

The Southern Colonies

Map #: 017

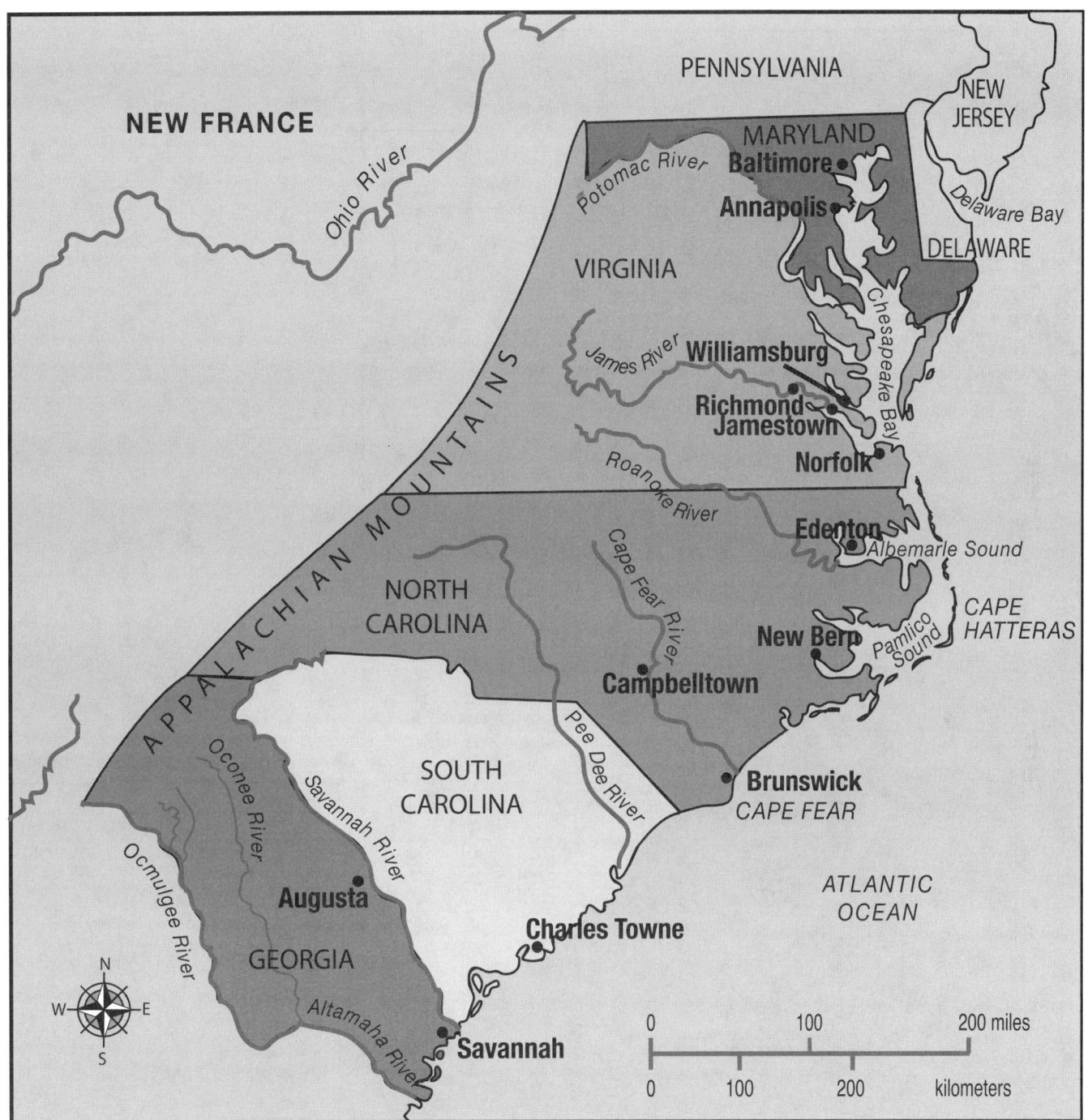

Maps for U.S. History — Economics of the British Colonies

Economics of the British Colonies

Map #: 018

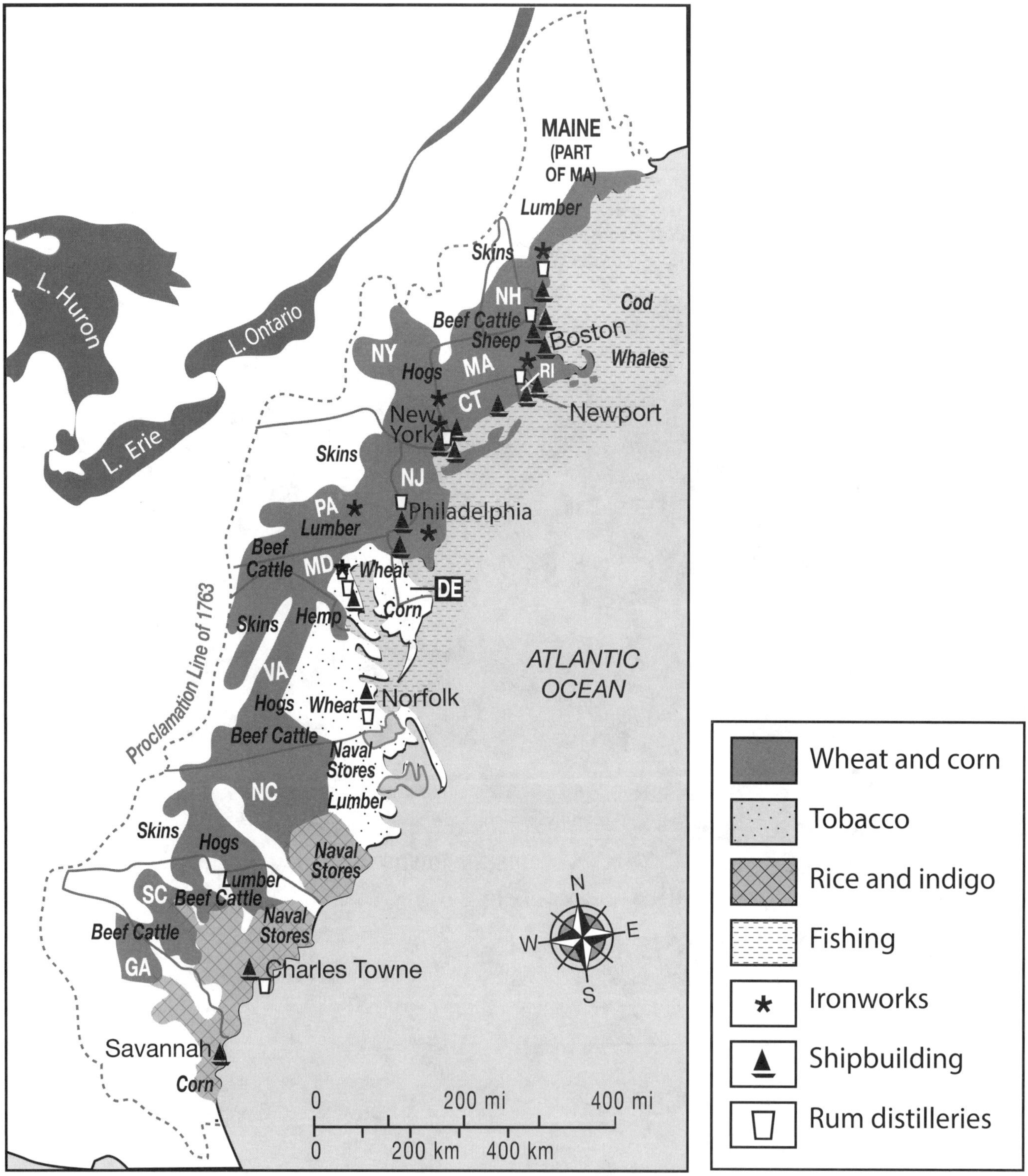

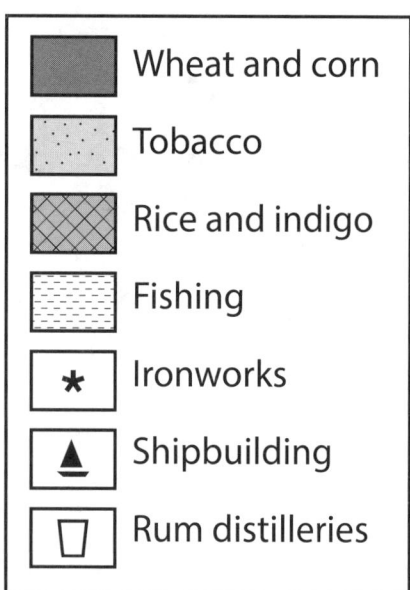

Name: _____ Date: _____

French, Spanish, and English Land Claims Prior to the French and Indian War

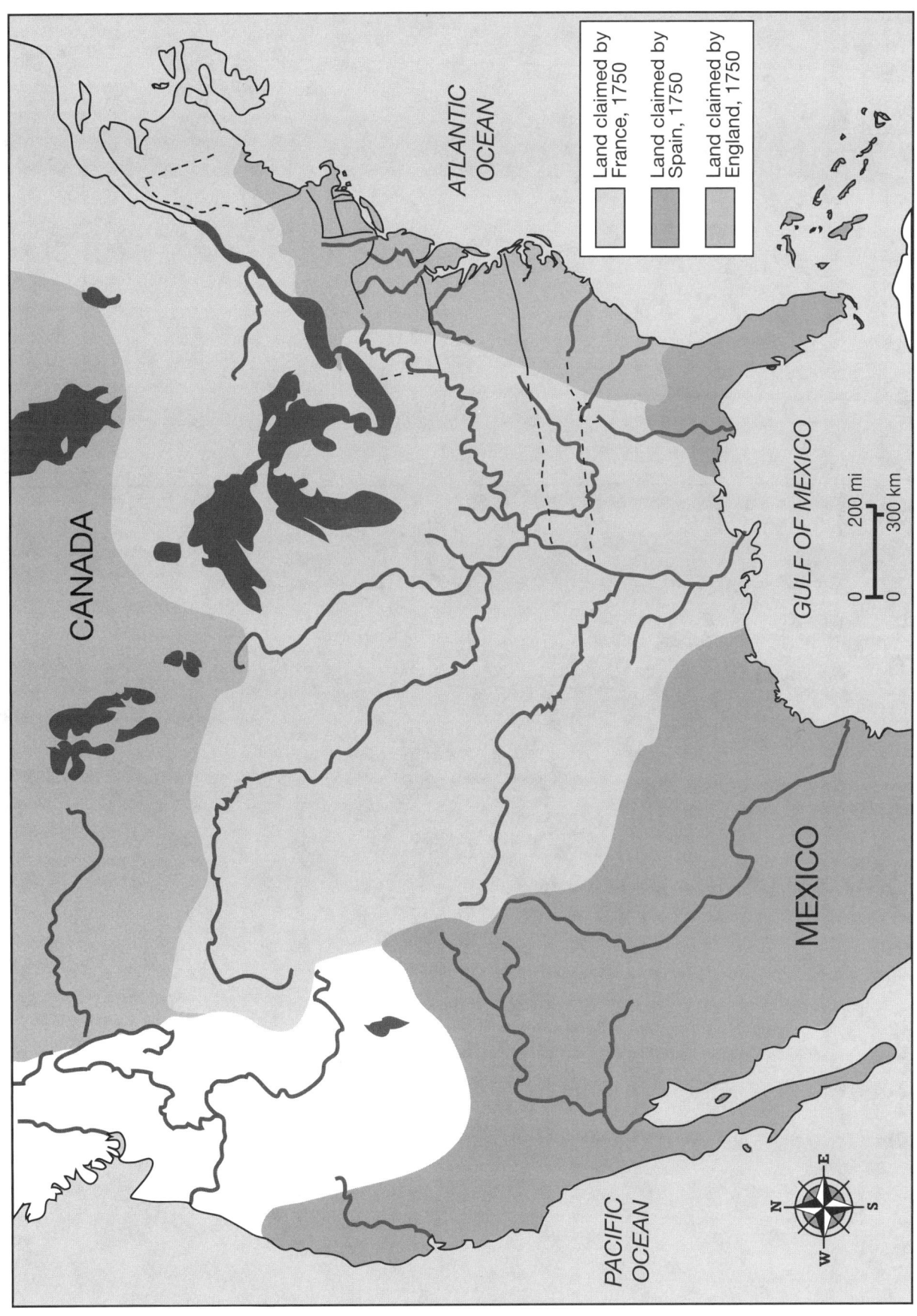

Name: _____ Date: _____

Land Taken From Native Americans, Before 1750–1810

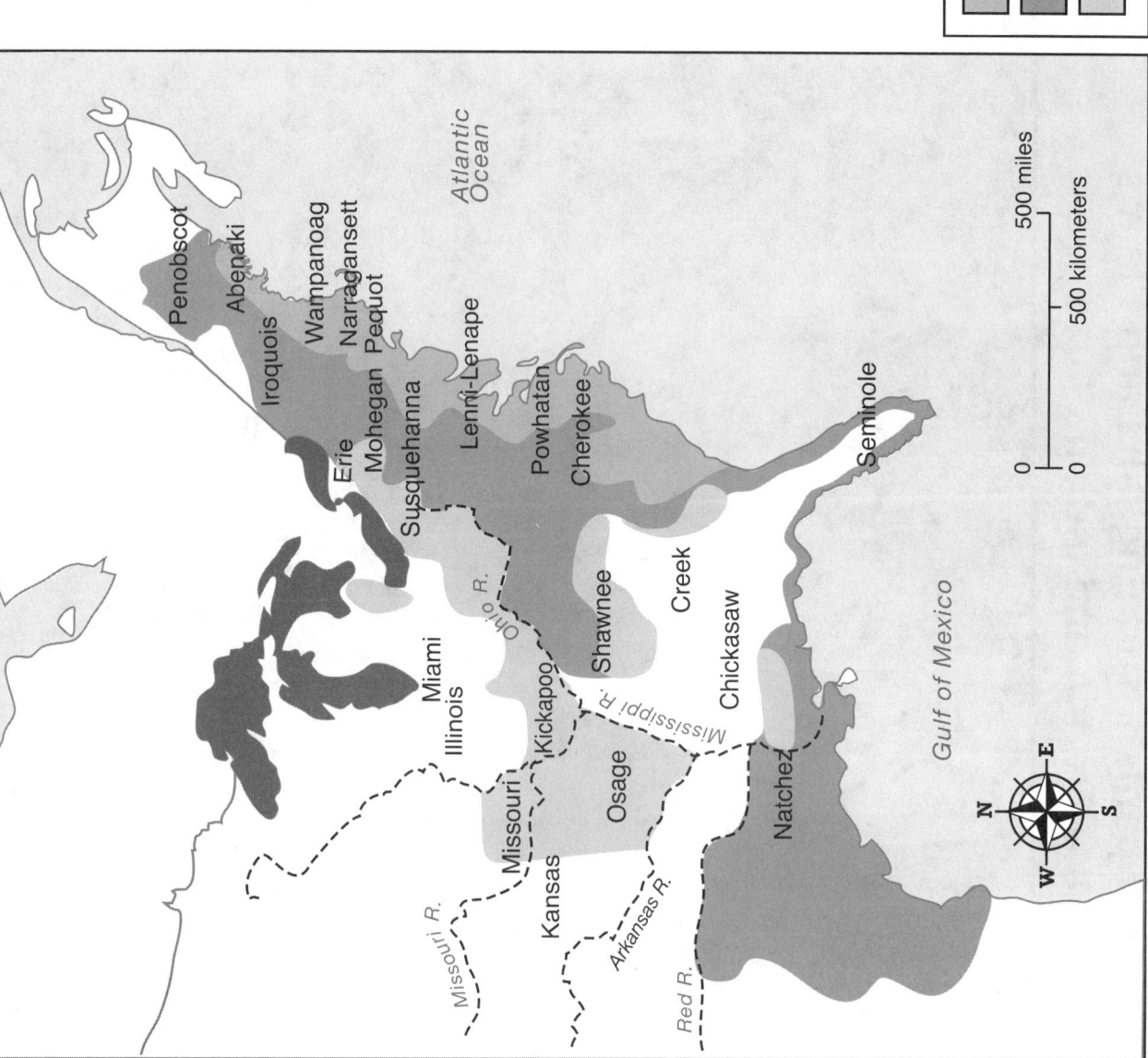

Name: _____ Date: _____

The French and Indian War, 1754–1763: French and British Forts

Maps for U.S. History — The French and Indian War, 1754–1763: French and British Forts

Map #: 021

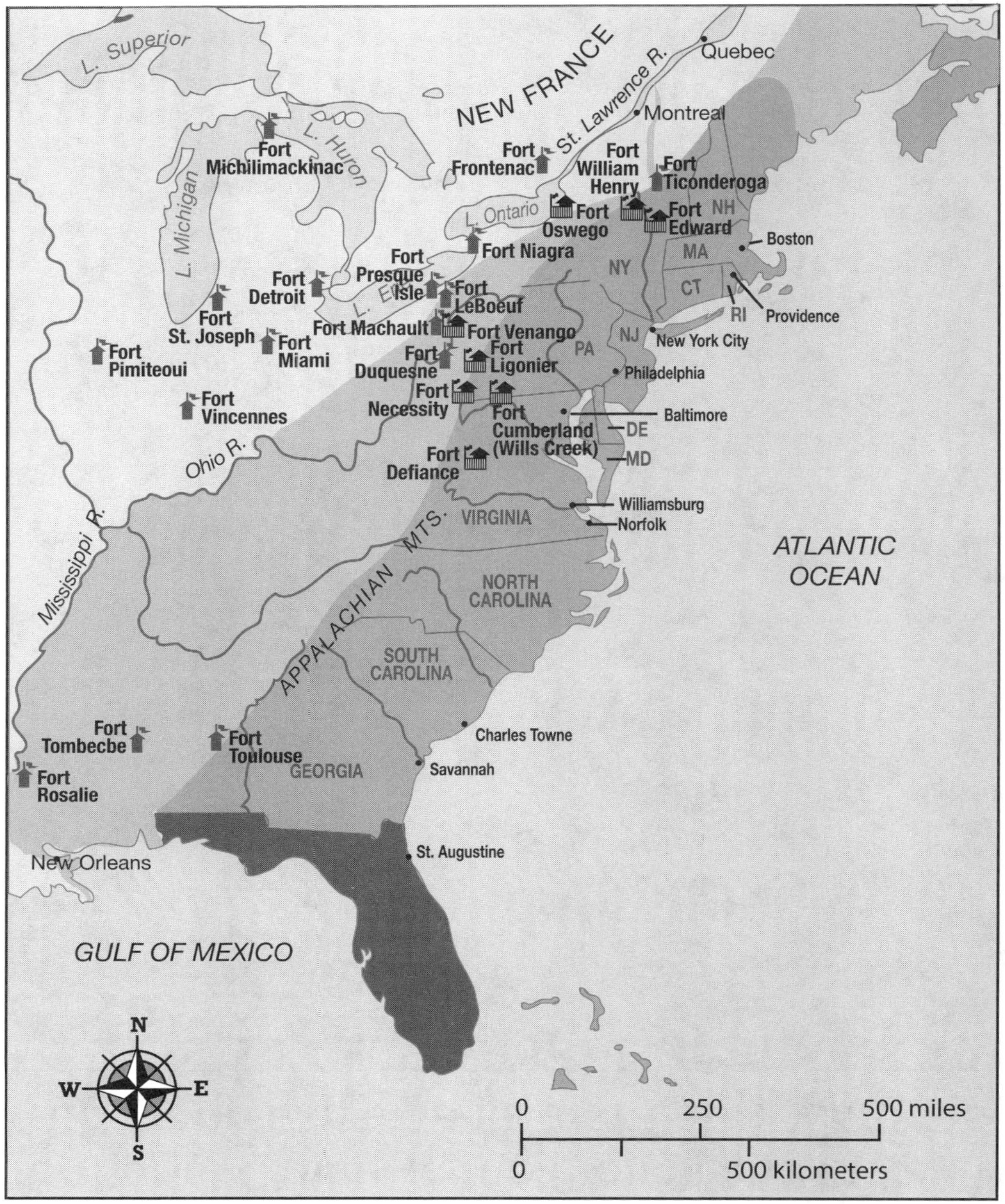

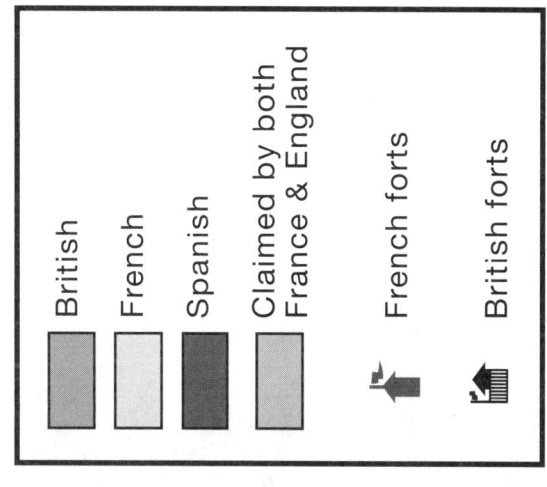

Name: _____ Date: _____

Maps for U.S. History   Territorial Claims in the French and Indian War, 1754–1763 Troop Movement/Battle Victories

Map #: 022

Territorial Claims in the French and Indian War, 1754–1763 With Troop Movements and Battle Victories

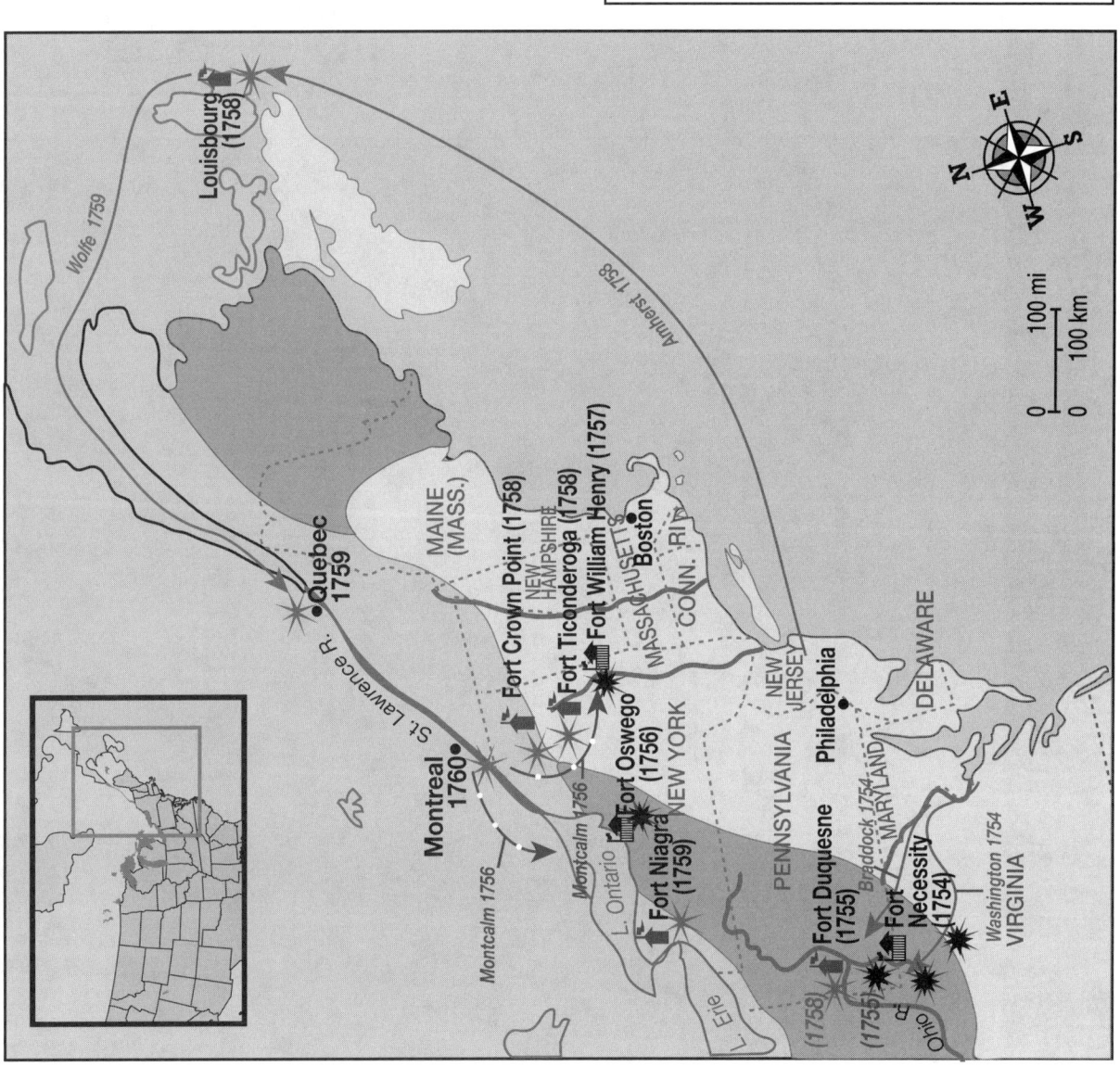

Maps for U.S. History

The Proclamation Line of 1763

Map #: 023

Map #: 024

Name: ____________________ Date: ____________________

Treaty of Paris, 1763

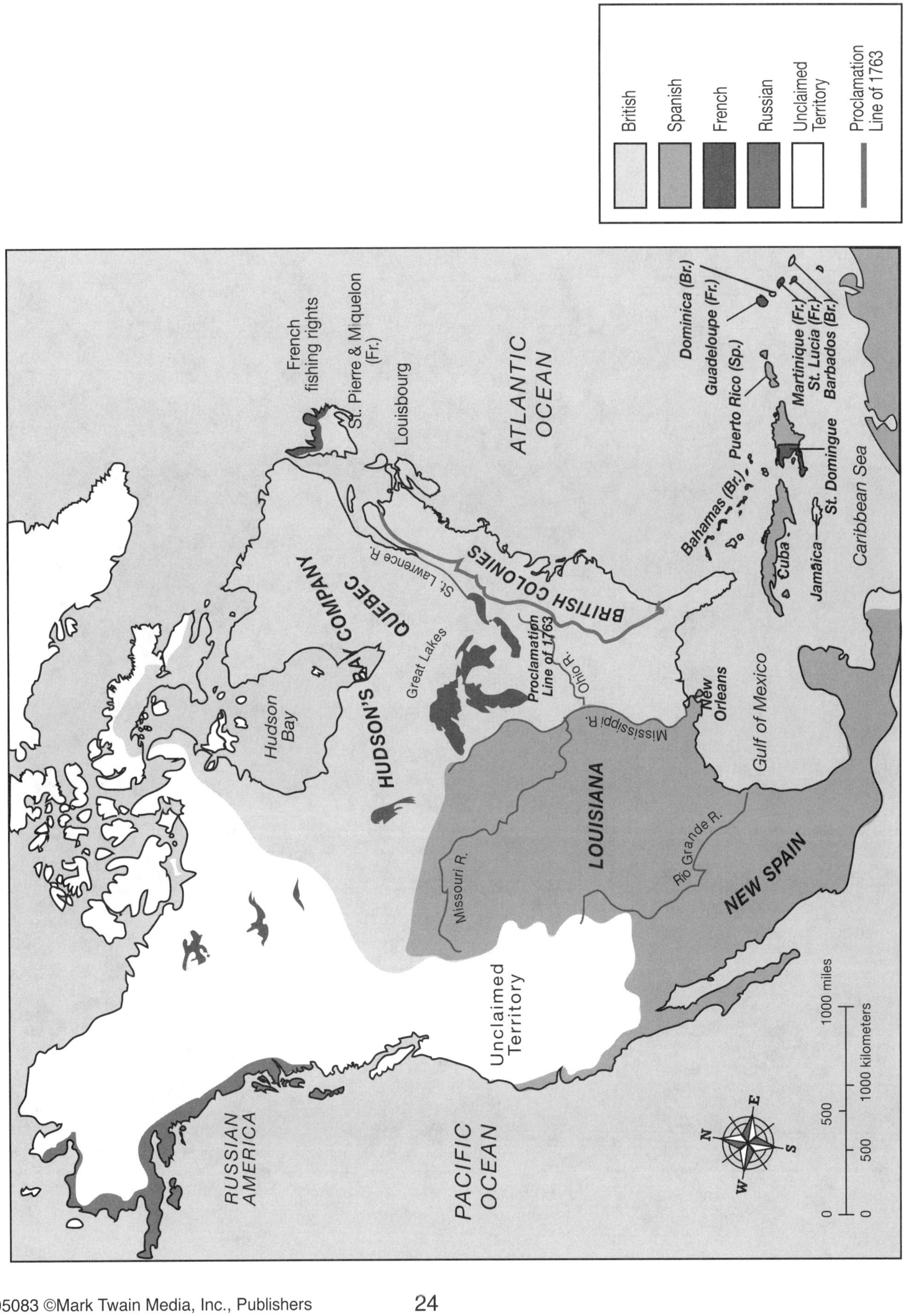

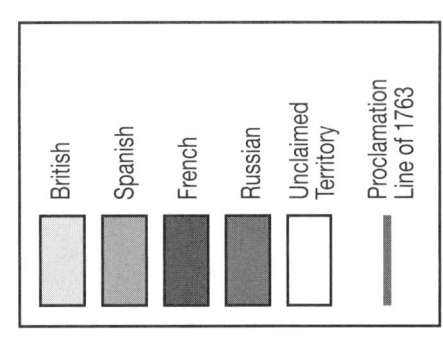

Name: _____ Date: _____

Midnight Rides of Paul Revere, William Dawes, and Samuel Prescott: All Routes

Maps for U.S. History — Midnight Rides of Paul Revere, William Dawes, and Samuel Prescott: All Routes

Map #: 025

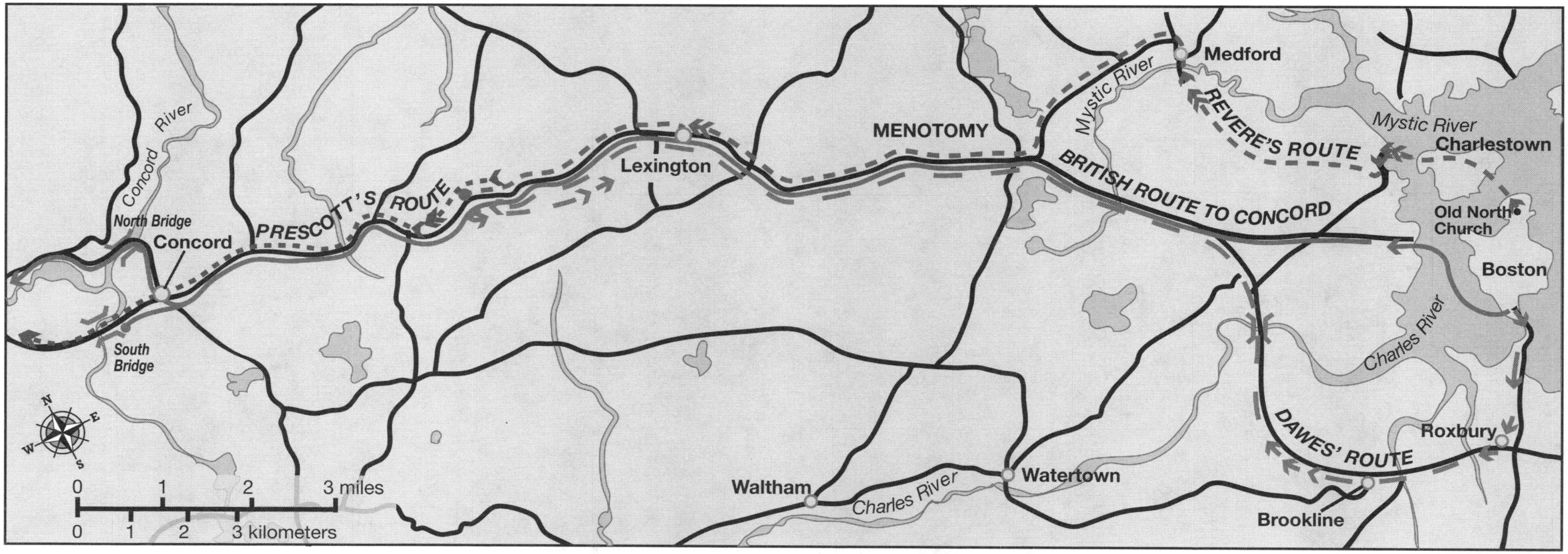

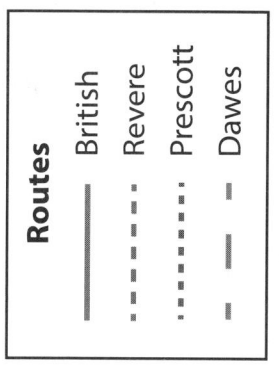

Name: _____
Date: _____

Battles of Lexington and Concord, April 18–19, 1775

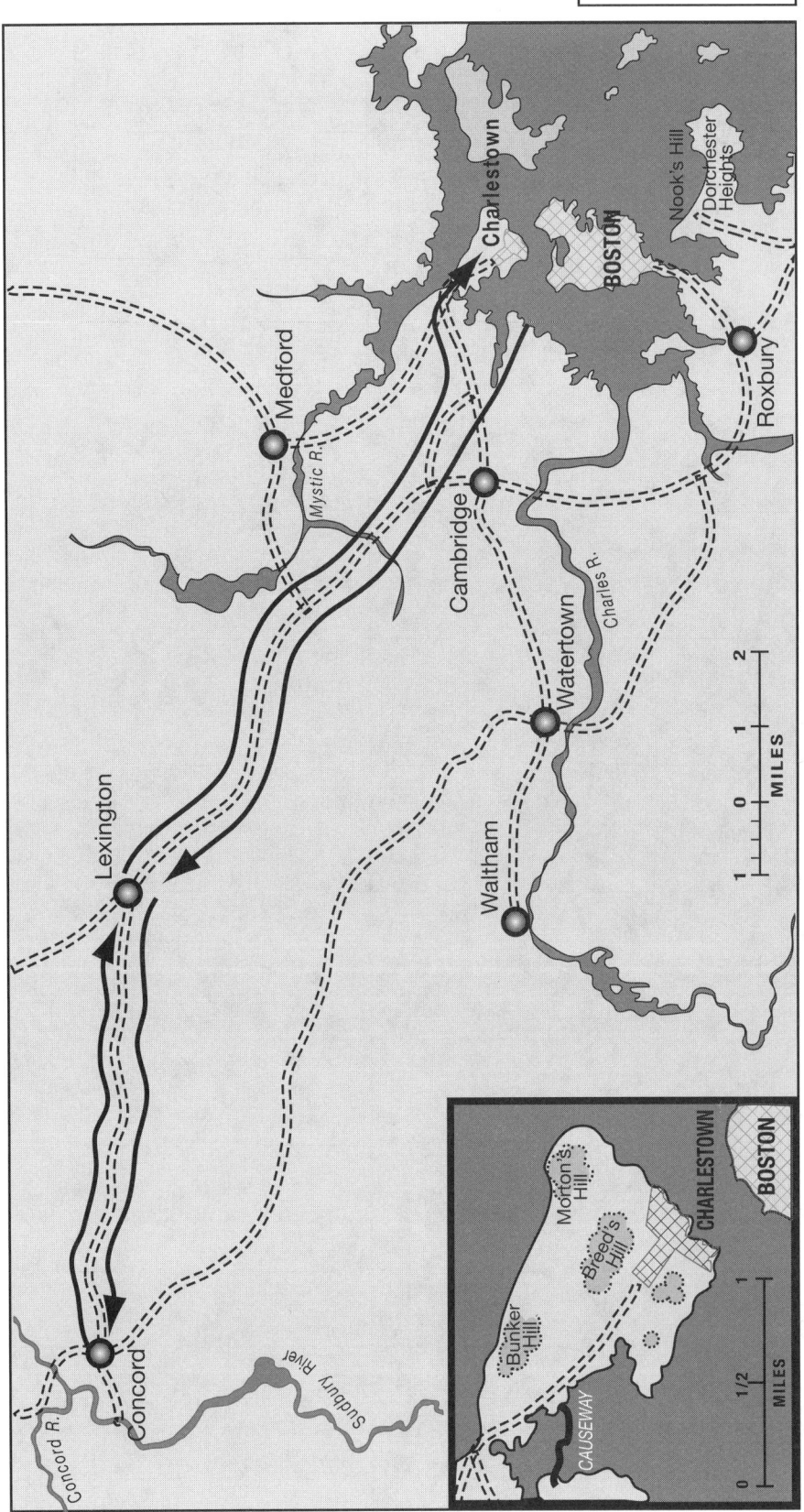

Maps for U.S. History

Name: _____ Date: _____

Battles of the American Revolution

Map #: 027

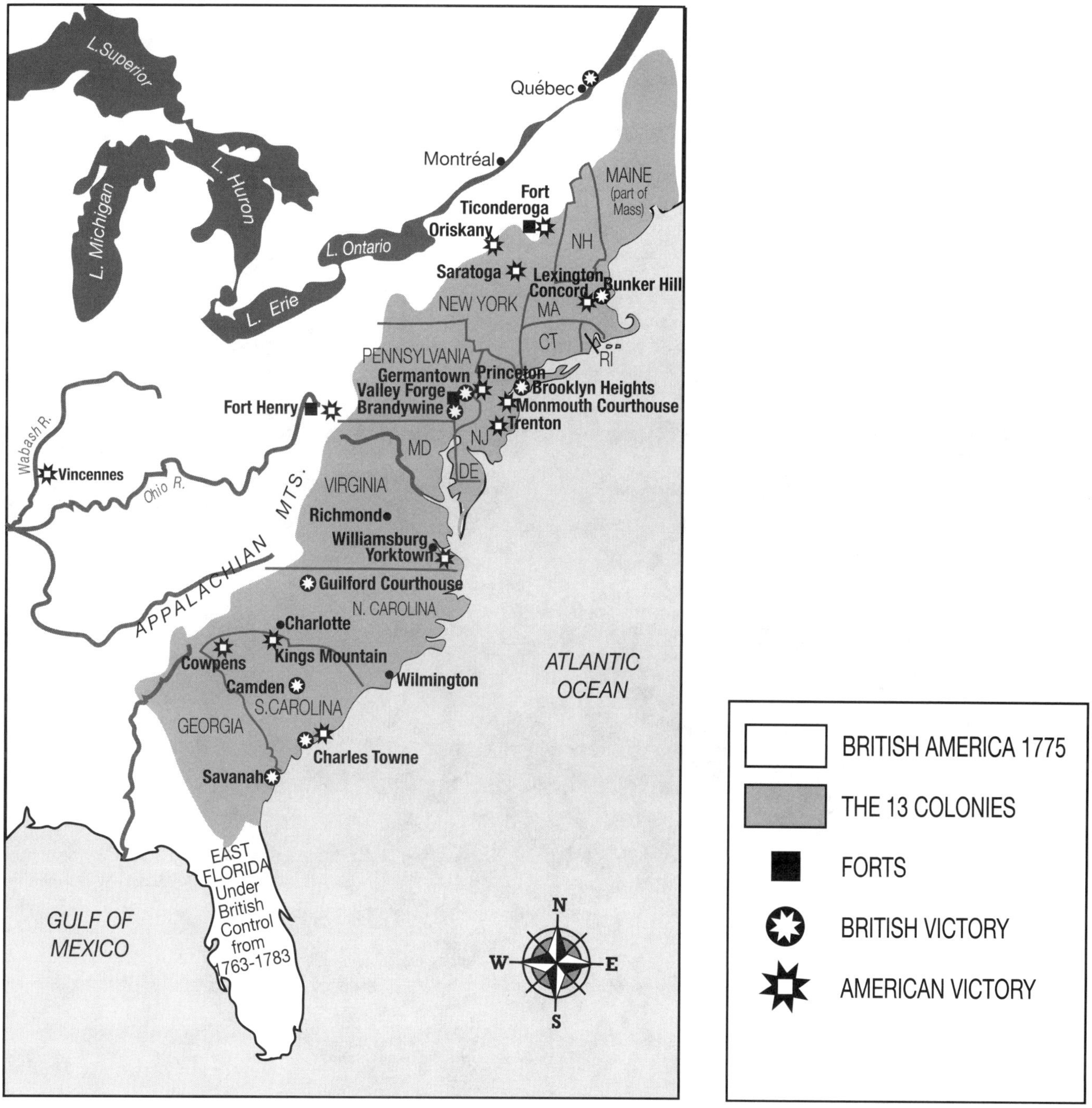

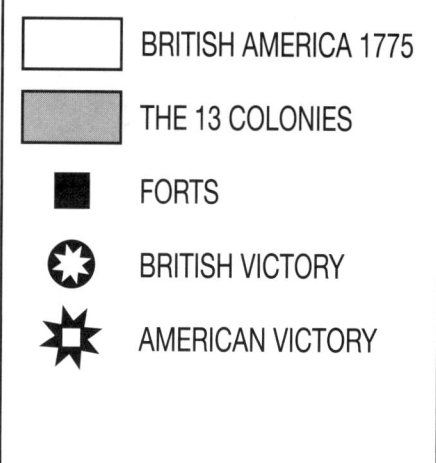

Maps for U.S. History

Treaty of Paris, 1783

Map #: 028

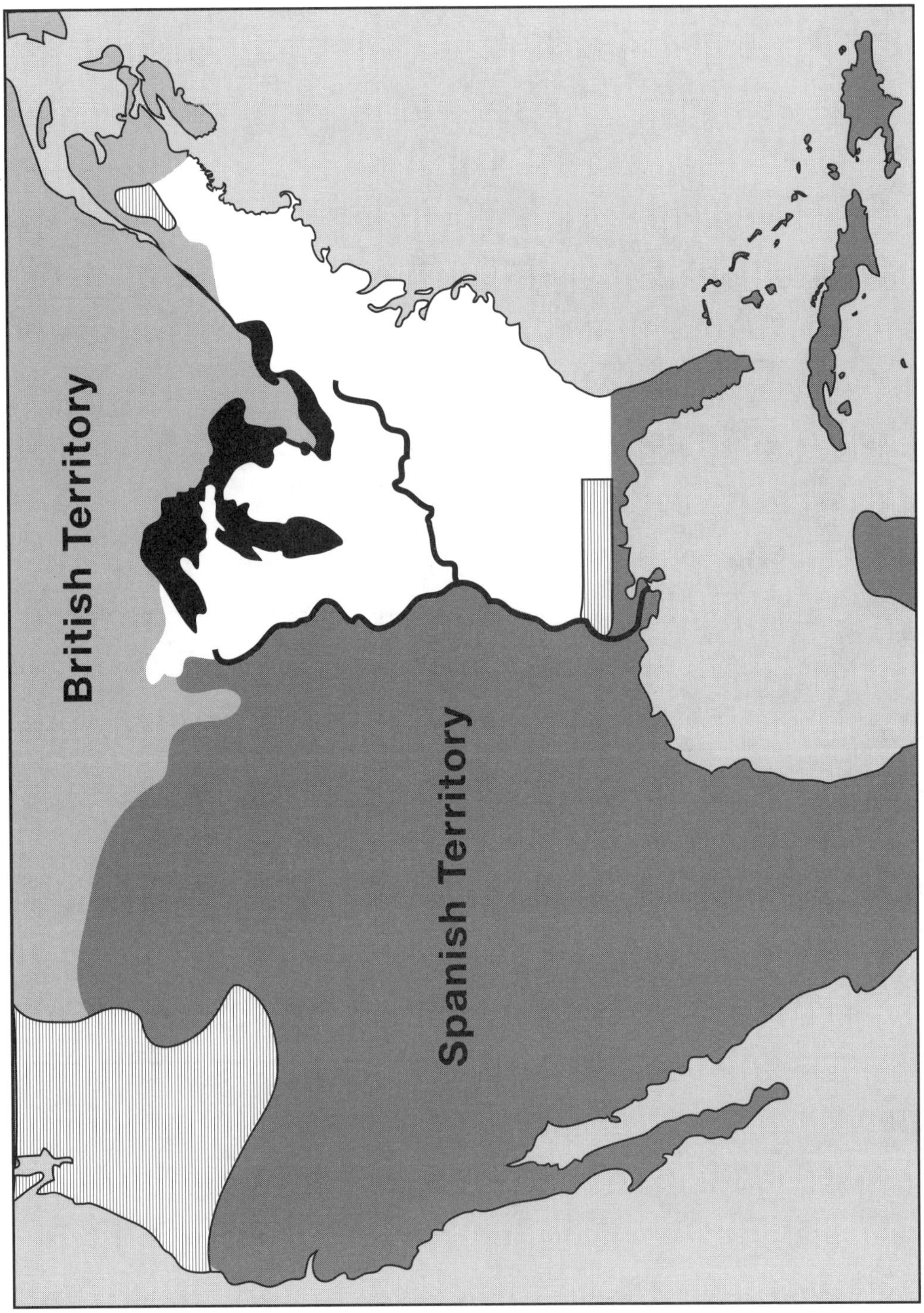

Name: _____
Date: _____

Treaty of Paris, 1783

United States after Treaty of Paris, 1783

Areas in dispute

British Territory

Spanish Territory

Territorial Acquisitions, 1783–1853

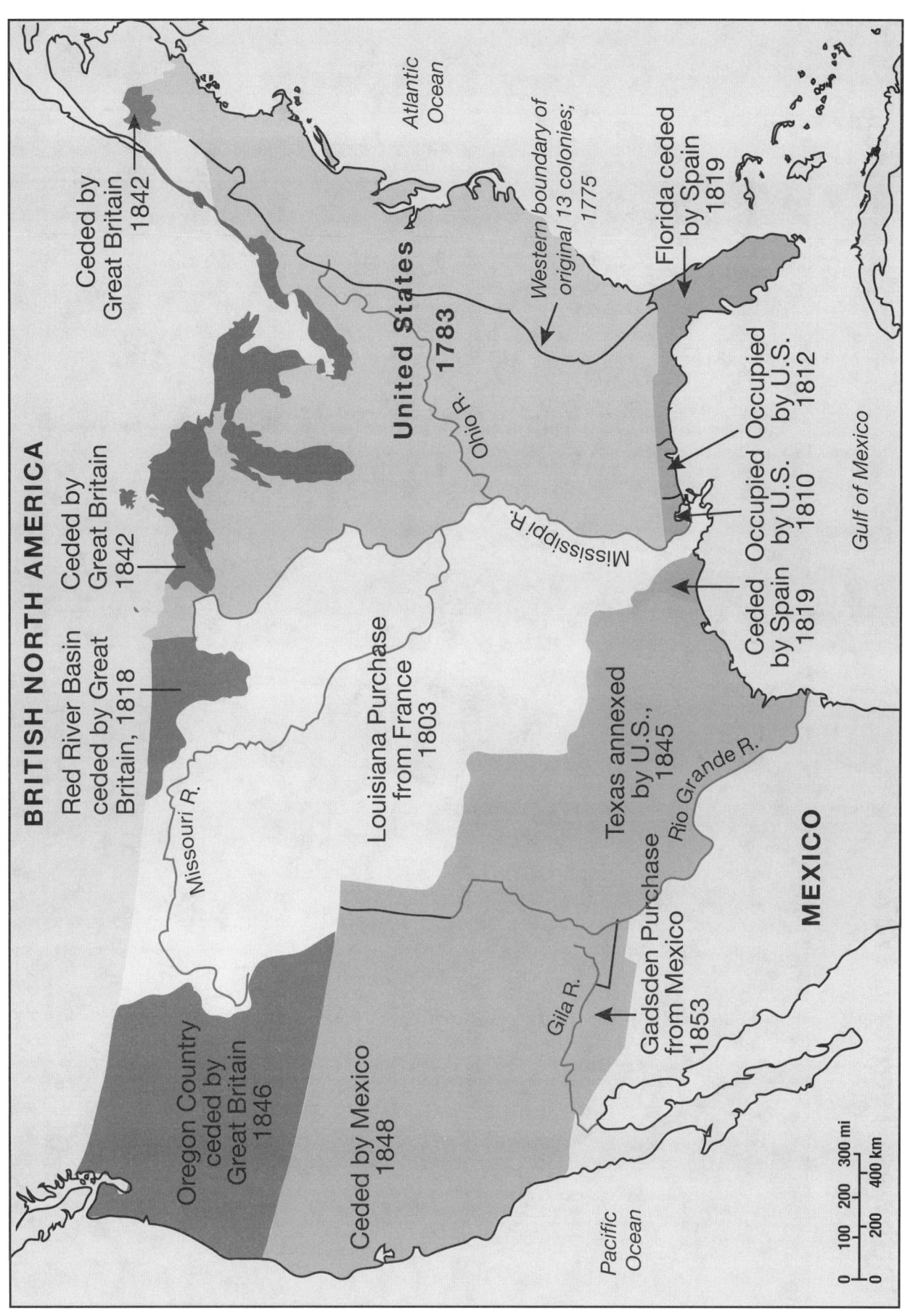

Name: _____ Date: _____

Northwest Territory, 1787

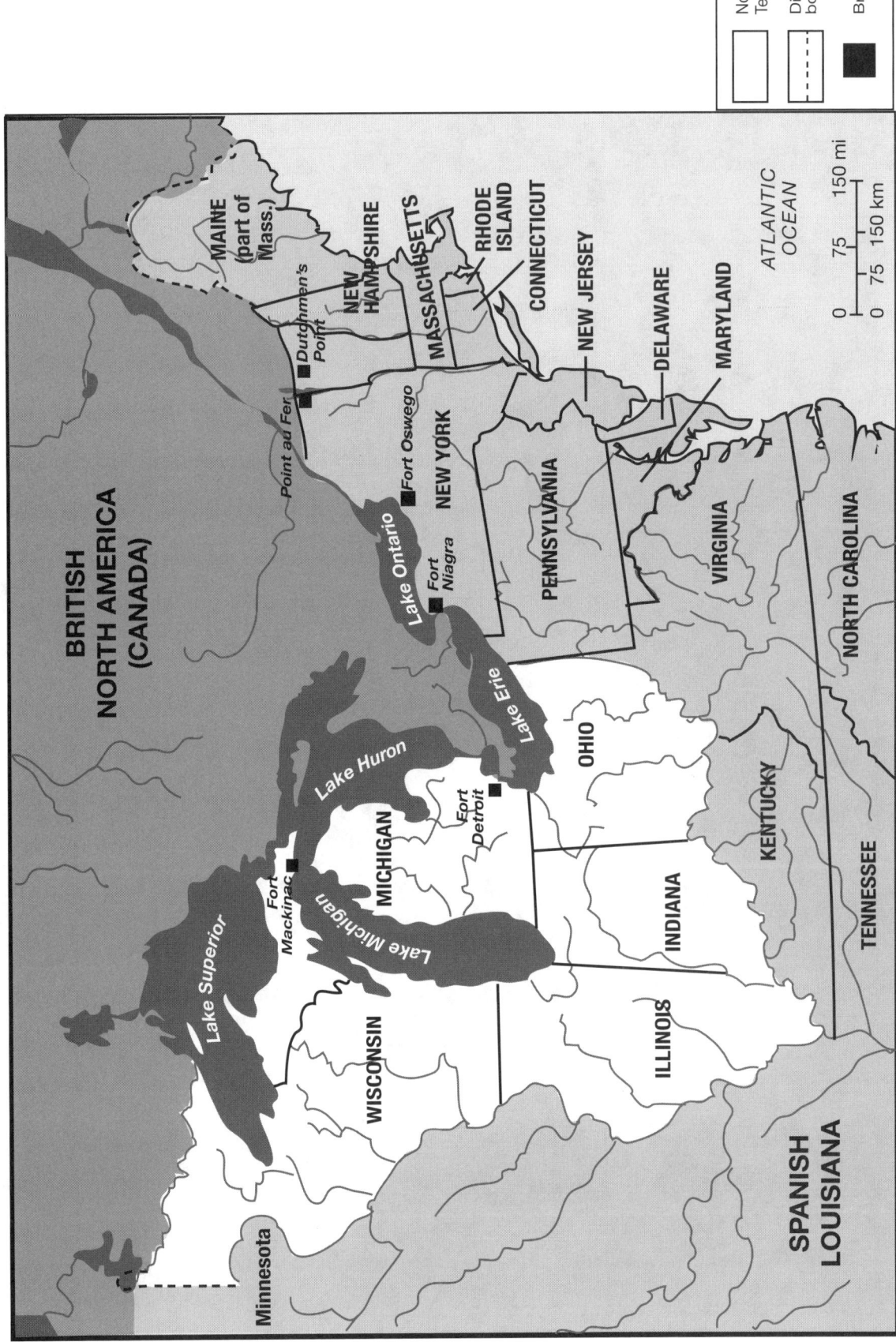

Name: _____ Date: _____

Maps for U.S. History   Early Roads to the West

Map #: 031

Early Roads to the West

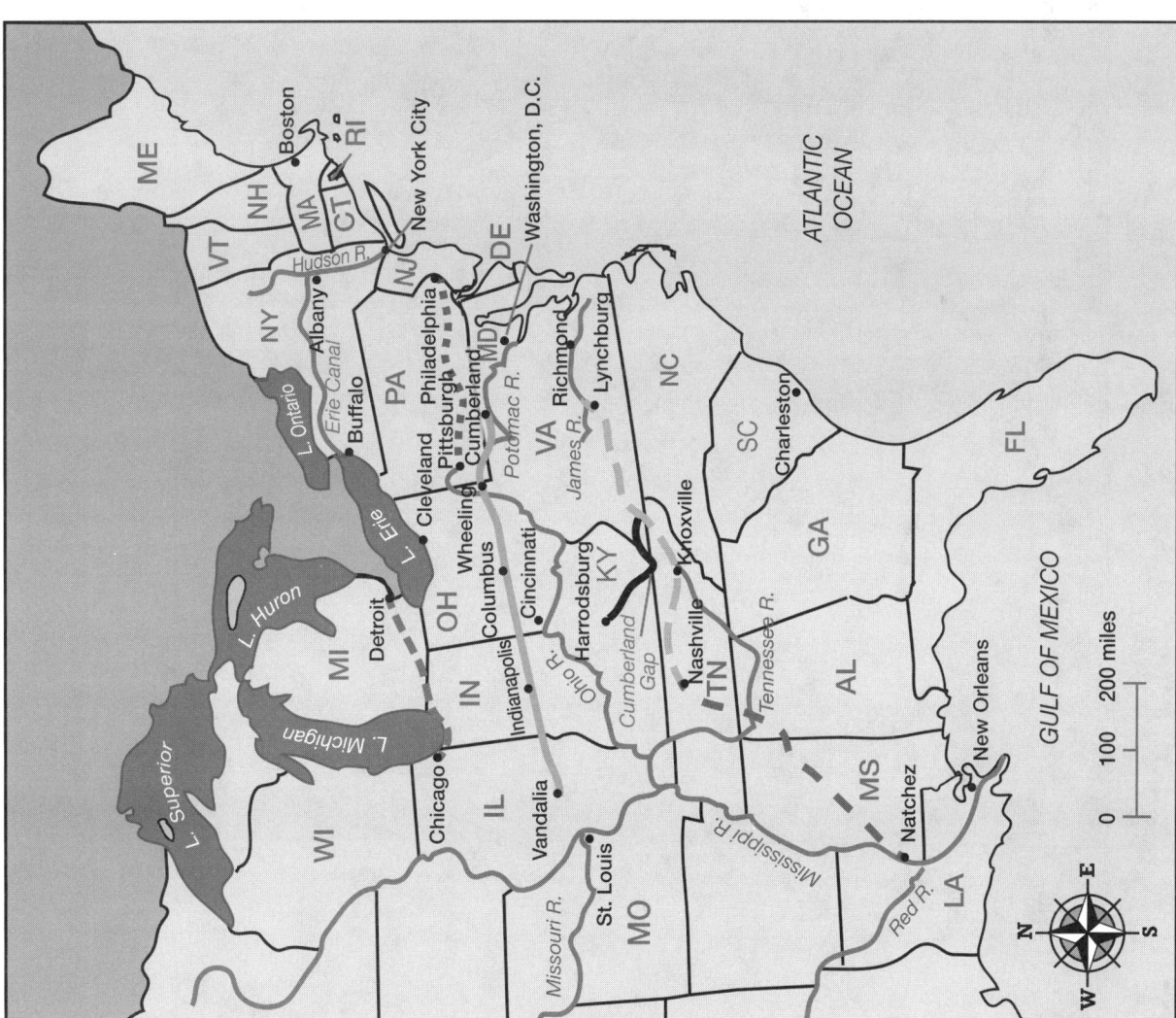

Name: _____
Date: _____

Louisiana Purchase, 1803

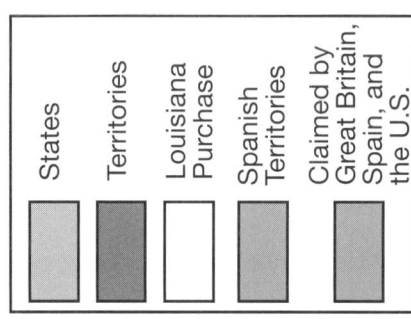

Map #: 032

Name: _____ Date: _____

Lewis and Clark Expedition, 1804–1806

Maps for U.S. History
Lewis and Clark Expedition, 1804–1806

Map #: 033

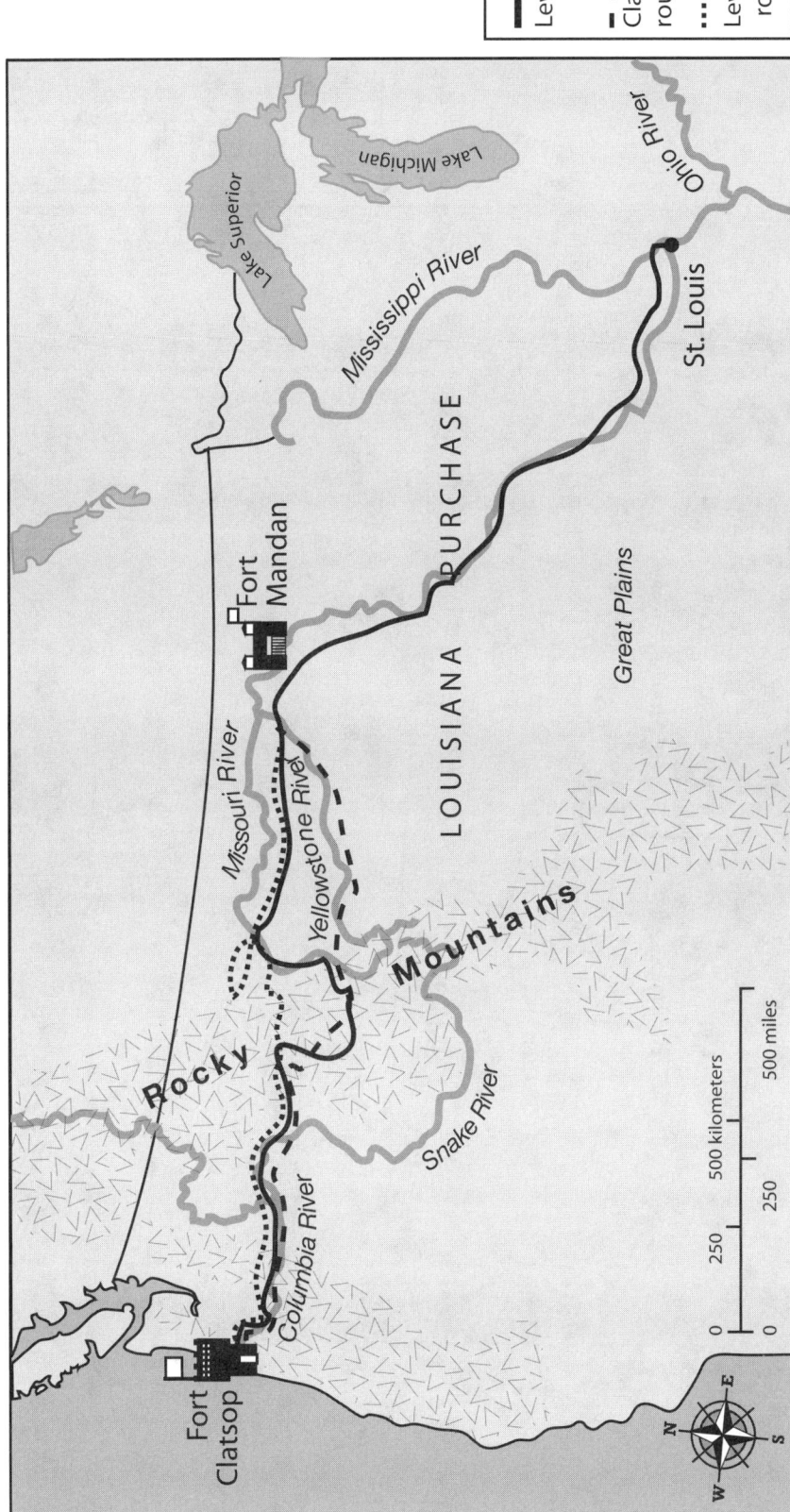

Name: _____ Date: _____

War of 1812 With Troop Movements and Battles

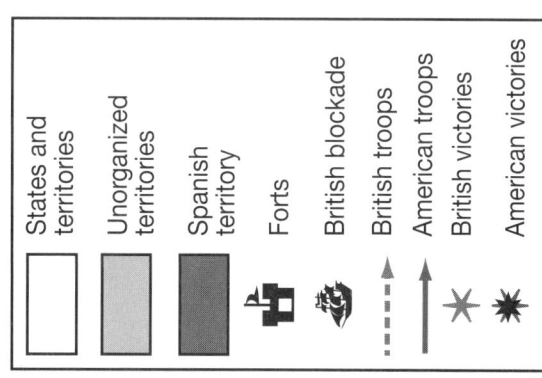

Maps for U.S. History
War of 1812 With Troop Movements and Battles

Map #: 034

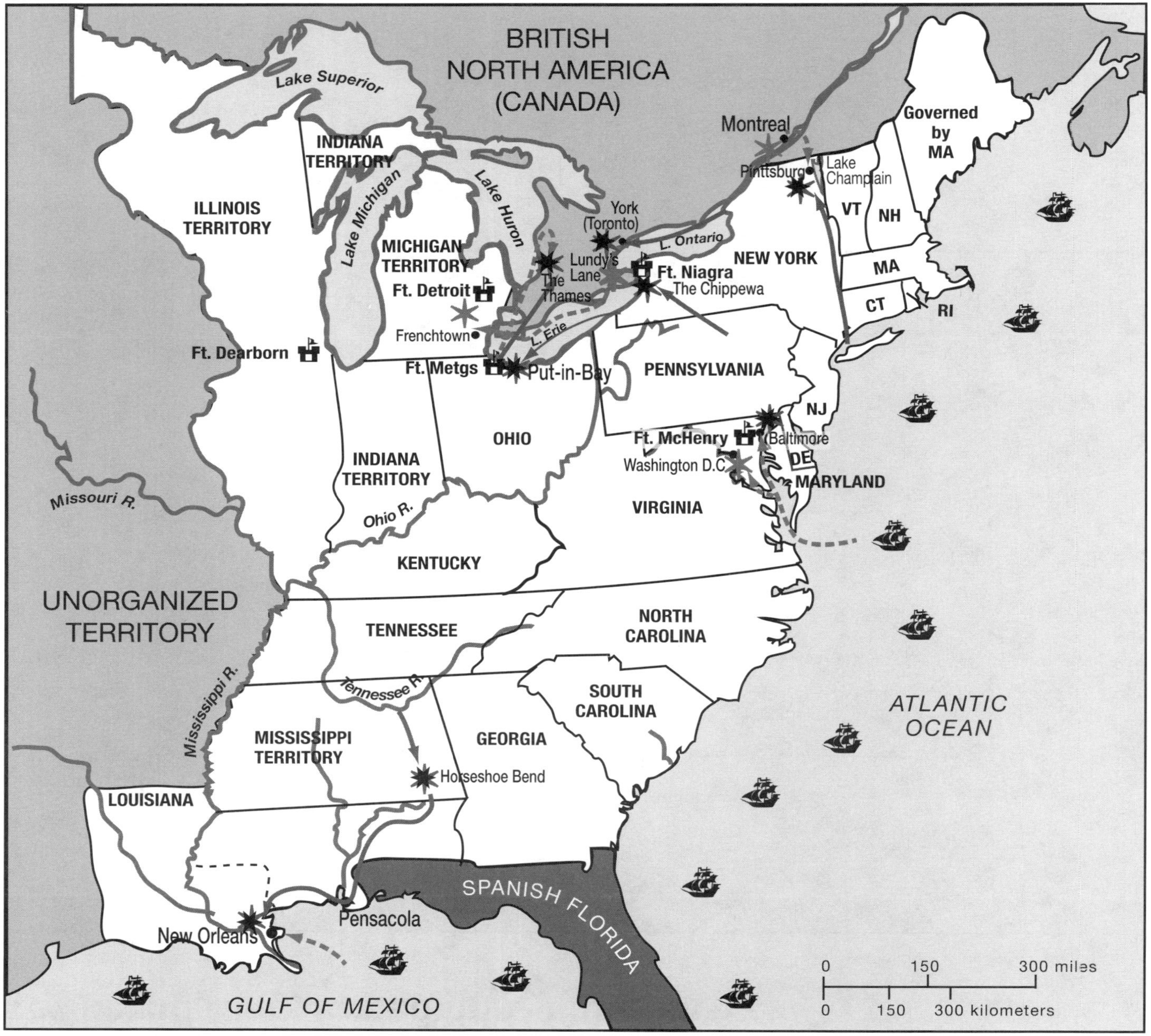

Maps for U.S. History

Westward Expansion, 1815–1845

Name: _____ Date: _____

Westward Expansion, 1815–1845

Map #: 035

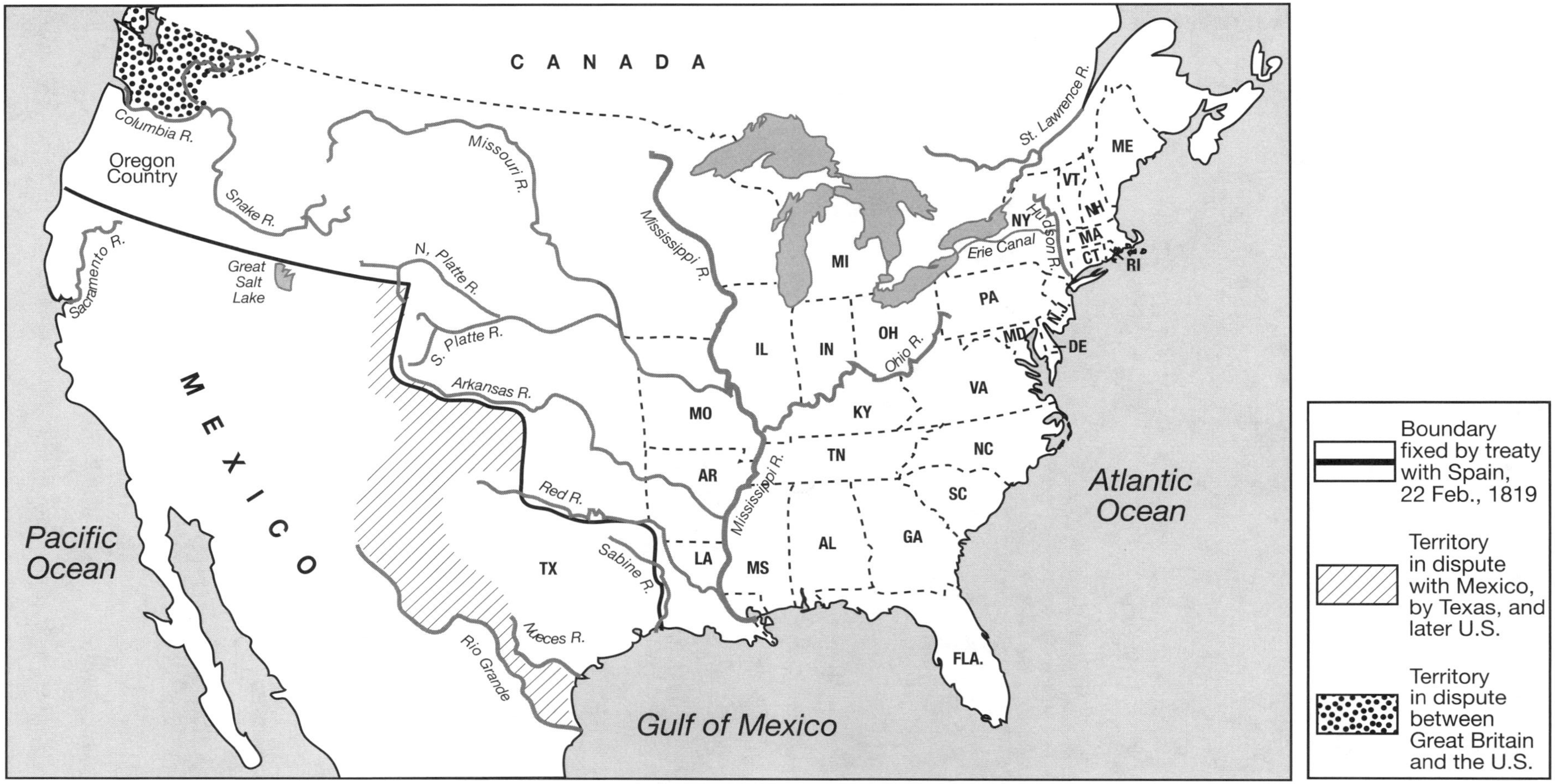

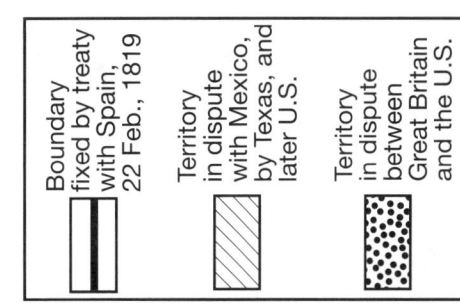

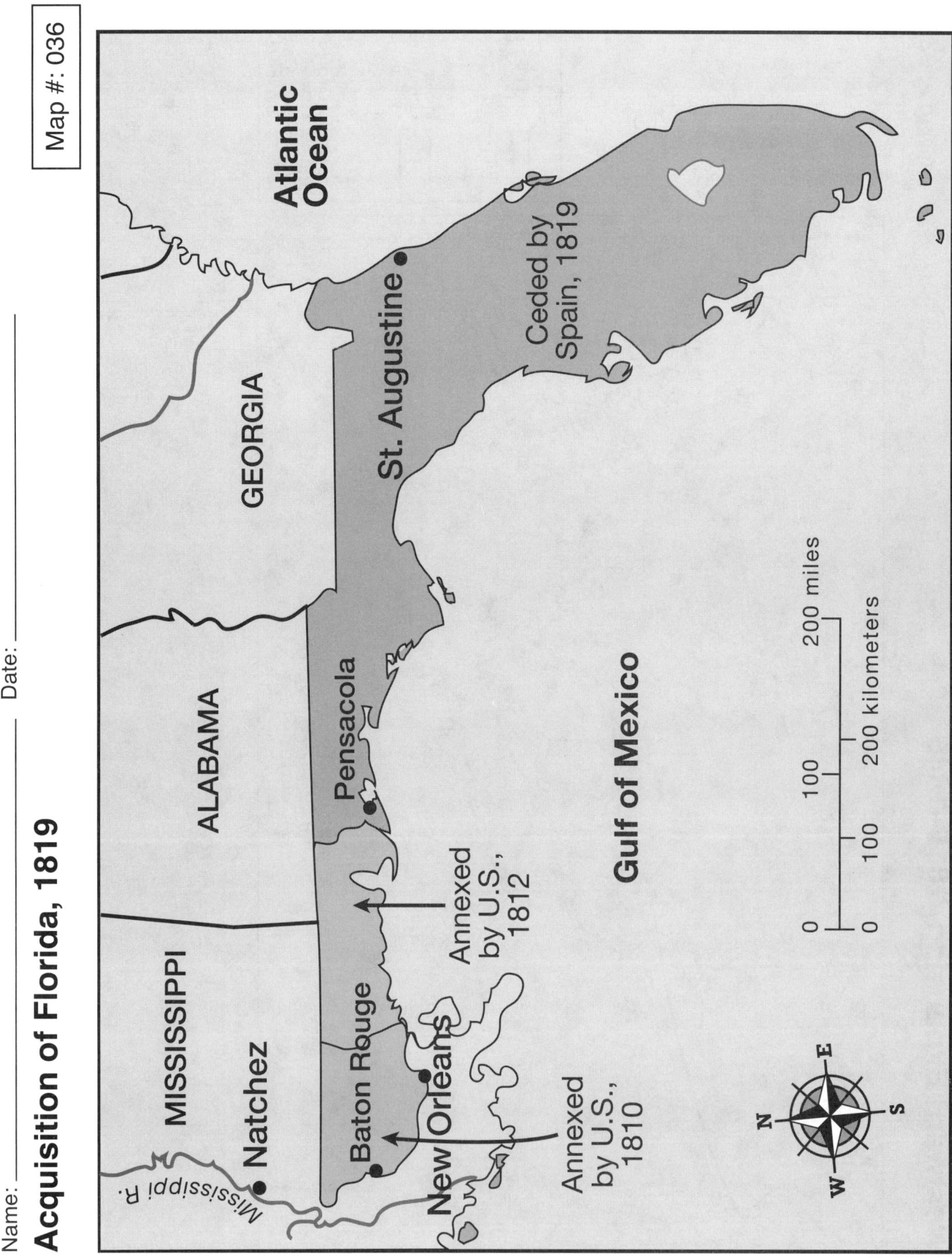

Name: _____ Date: _____

Missouri Compromise, 1820

Maps for U.S. History

Missouri Compromise, 1820

Map #: 037

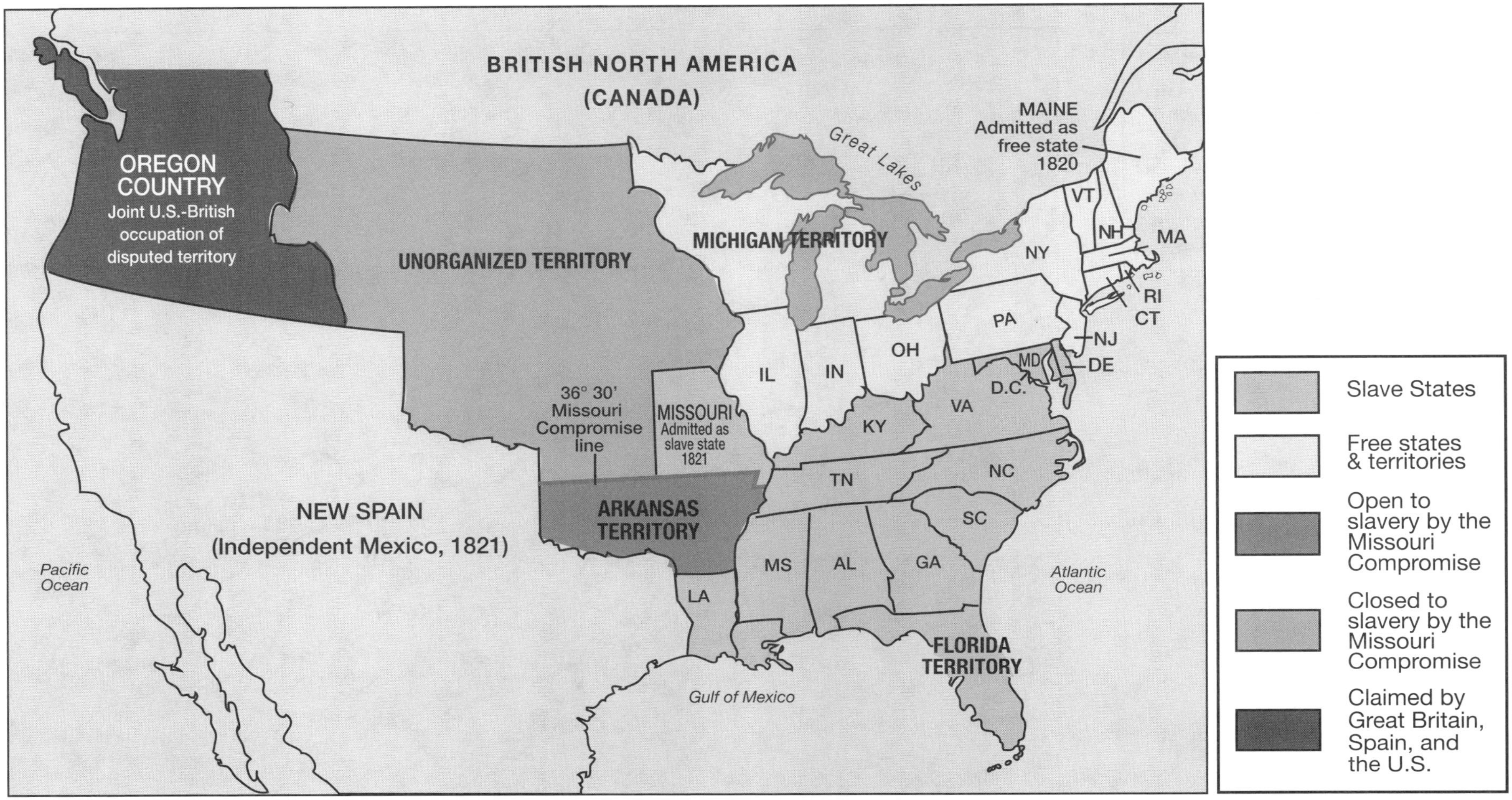

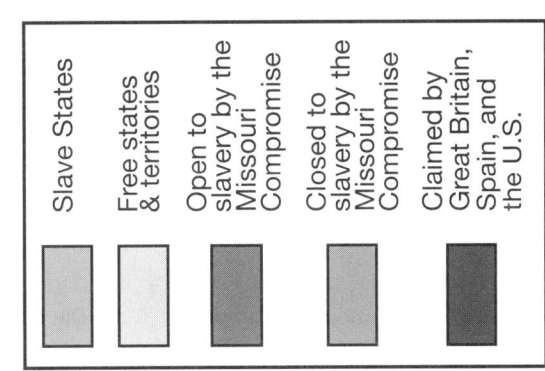

Legend:
- Slave States
- Free states & territories
- Open to slavery by the Missouri Compromise
- Closed to slavery by the Missouri Compromise
- Claimed by Great Britain, Spain, and the U.S.

Maps for U.S. History

Removal of Native Americans, 1820–1840

Map #: 038

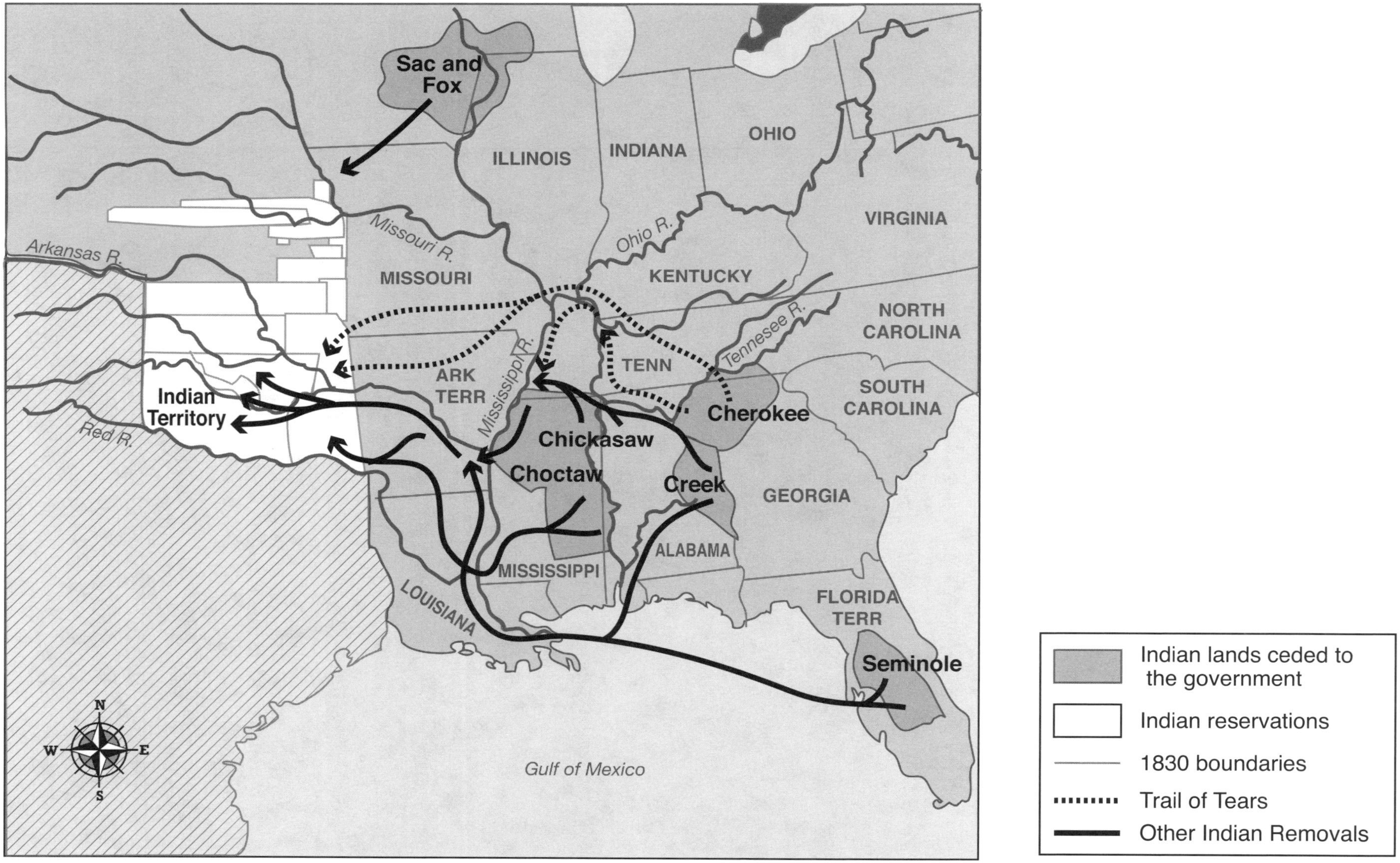

Name: _____ Date: _____

Removal of Native Americans, 1820–1840

Legend:
- Indian lands ceded to the government
- Indian reservations
- 1830 boundaries
- Trail of Tears
- Other Indian Removals

Tribes shown: Sac and Fox, Cherokee, Chickasaw, Choctaw, Creek, Seminole

States/Territories labeled: Ohio, Indiana, Illinois, Missouri, Kentucky, Virginia, Tennessee, North Carolina, South Carolina, Georgia, Alabama, Mississippi, Louisiana, Arkansas Territory, Florida Territory, Indian Territory

Rivers: Ohio R., Tennessee R., Mississippi R., Missouri R., Arkansas R., Red R.

Gulf of Mexico

Name: _____ Date: _____

Trail of Tears and the Cherokee Removal, 1830s

Maps for U.S. History

Trail of Tears and the Cherokee Removal, 1830s

Map #: 039

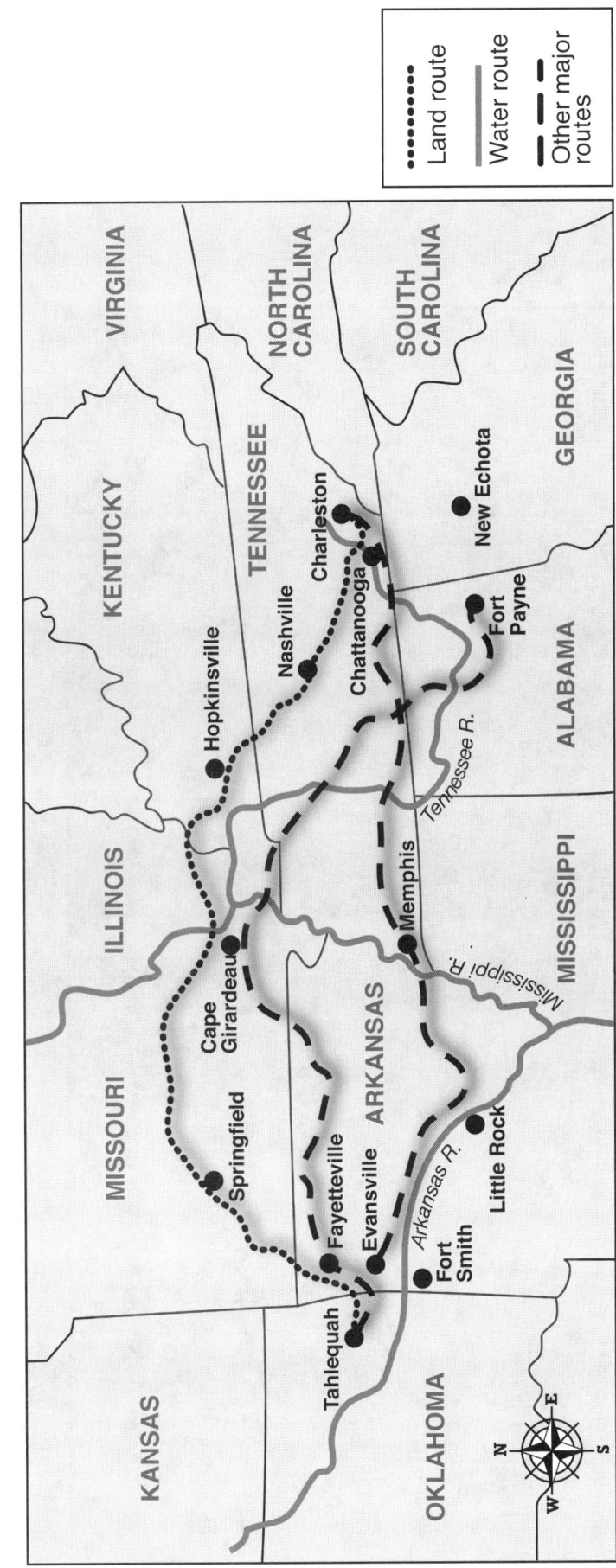

Name: _____
Date: _____

Western Trails

Maps for U.S. History

Map #: 040

Western Trails

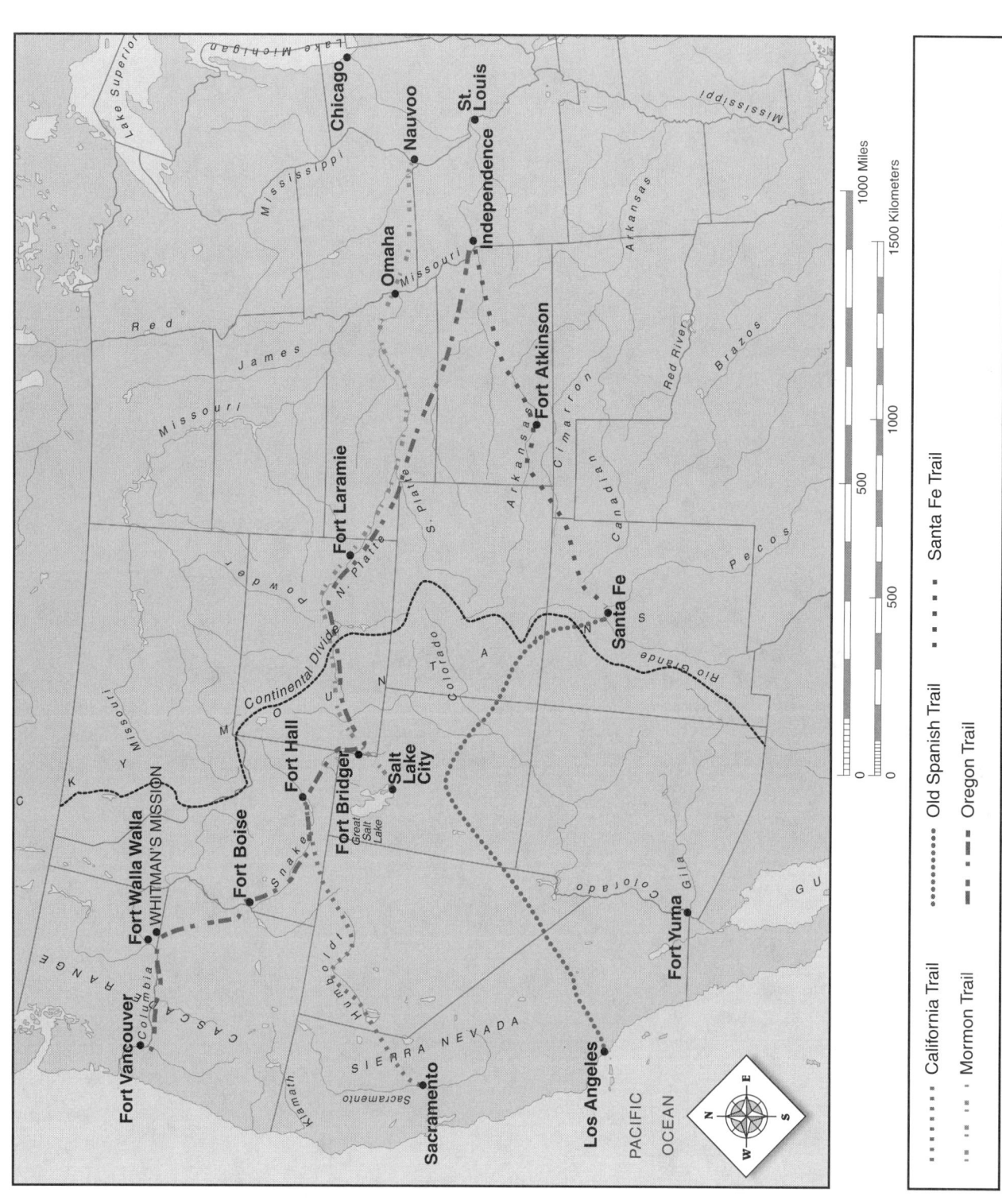

Name: _____ Date: _____

The Santa Fe Trail

Maps for U.S. History

Map #: 041

The Santa Fe Trail

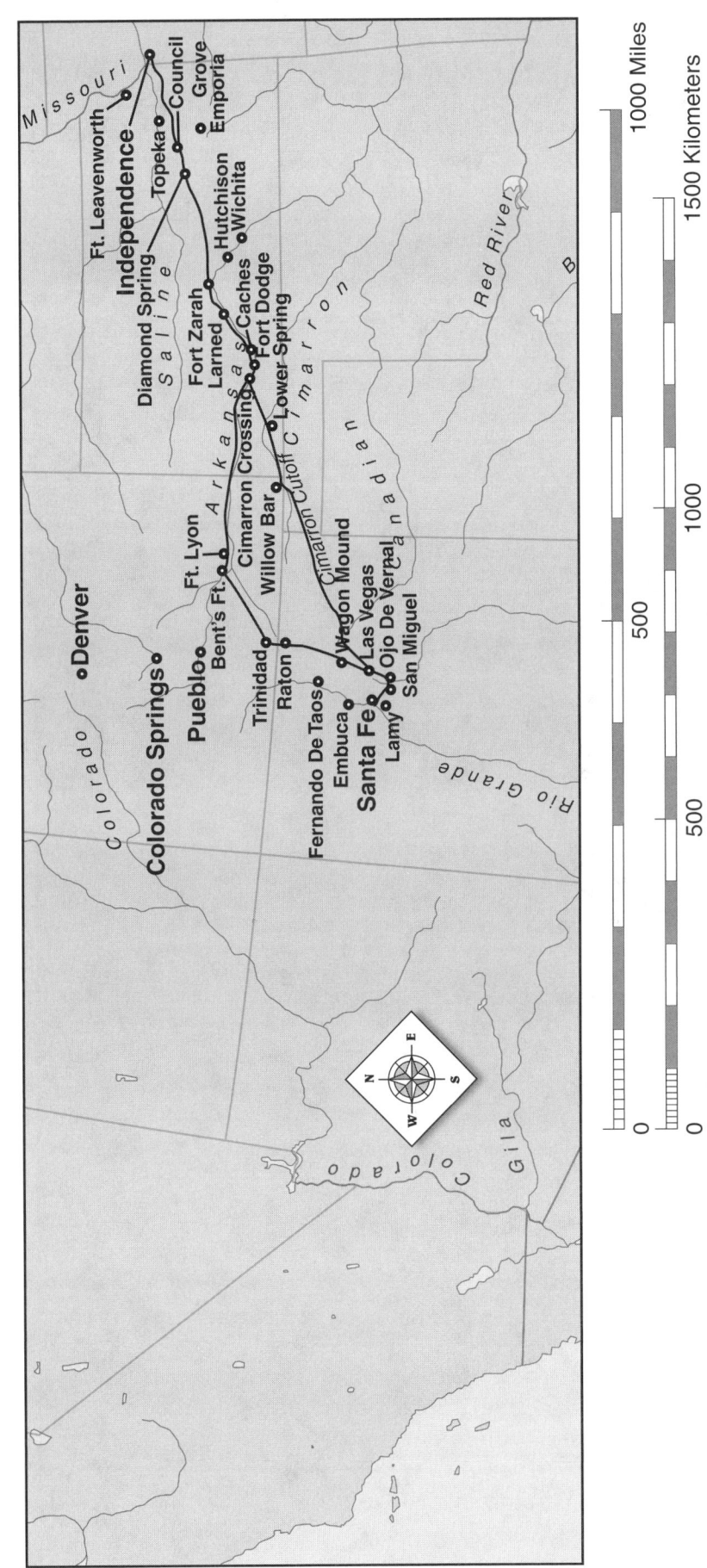

Name: _____

Date: _____

The Oregon Trail

Maps for U.S. History

The Oregon Trail

Map #: 042

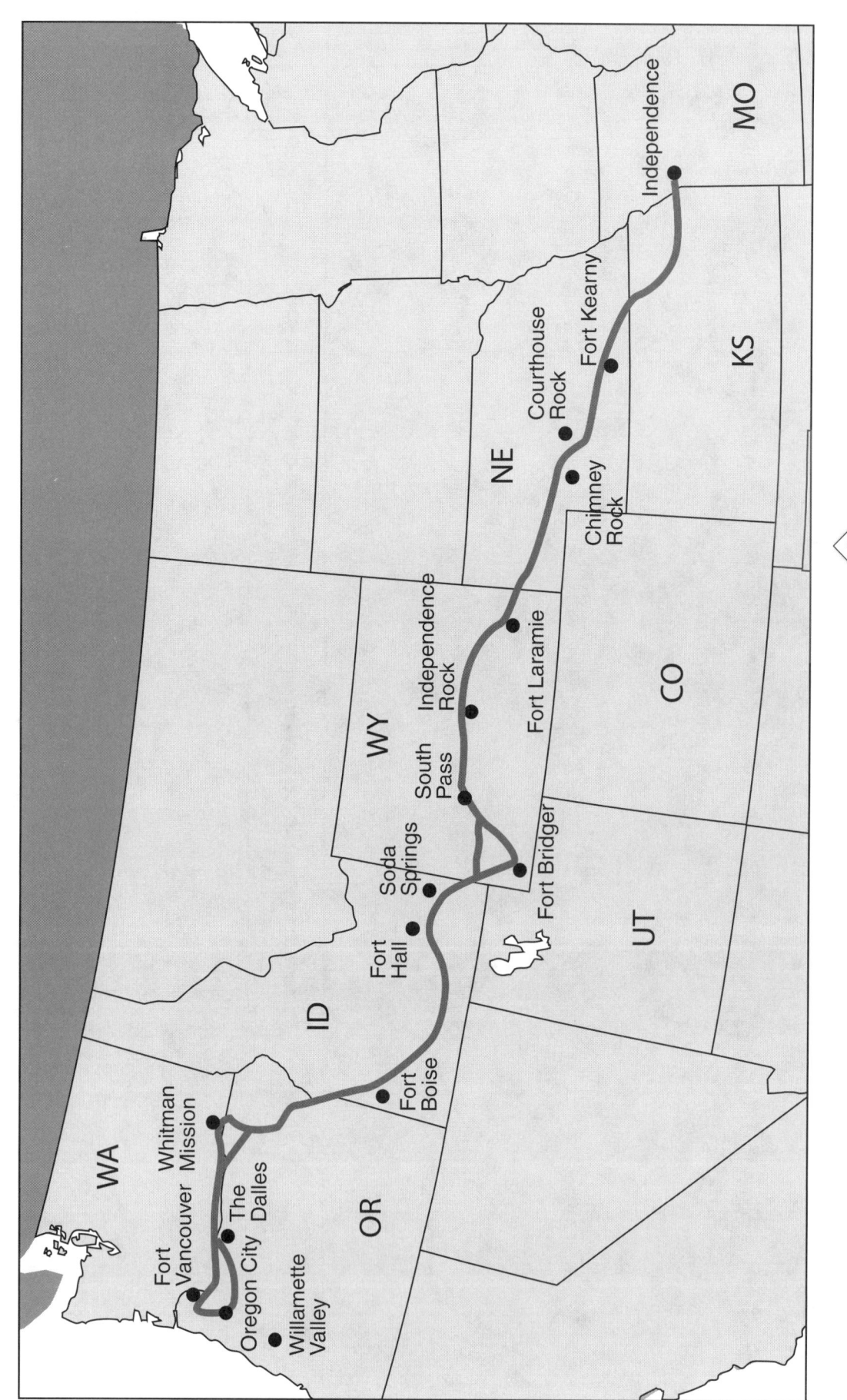

Maps for U.S. History

The Mormon Trail

Map #: 043

Name: _____ Date: _____

The Mormon Trail

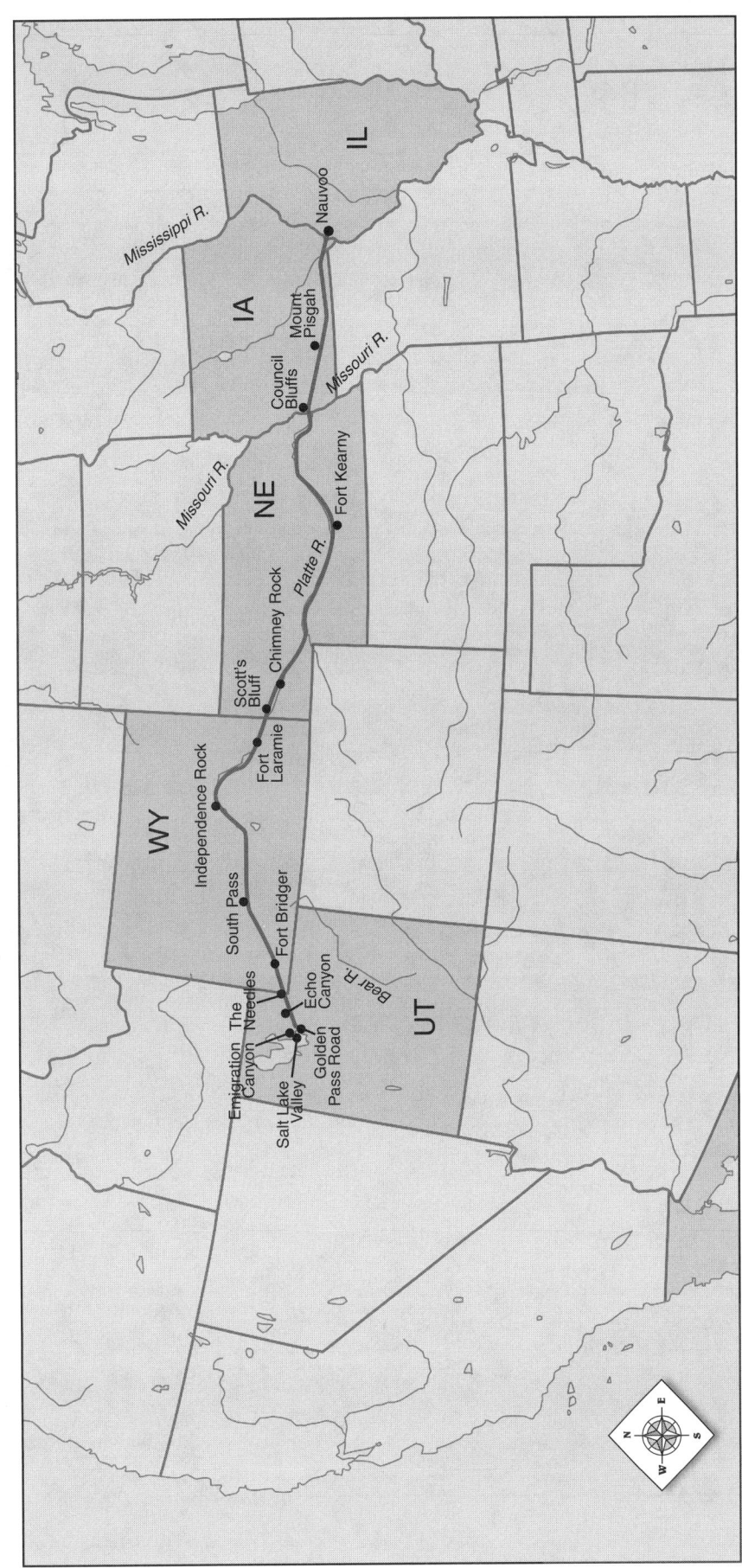

CD-405083 ©Mark Twain Media, Inc., Publishers

Maps for U.S. History

Important Canals, 1840

Name: _____ Date: _____

Important Canals, 1840

Map #: 044

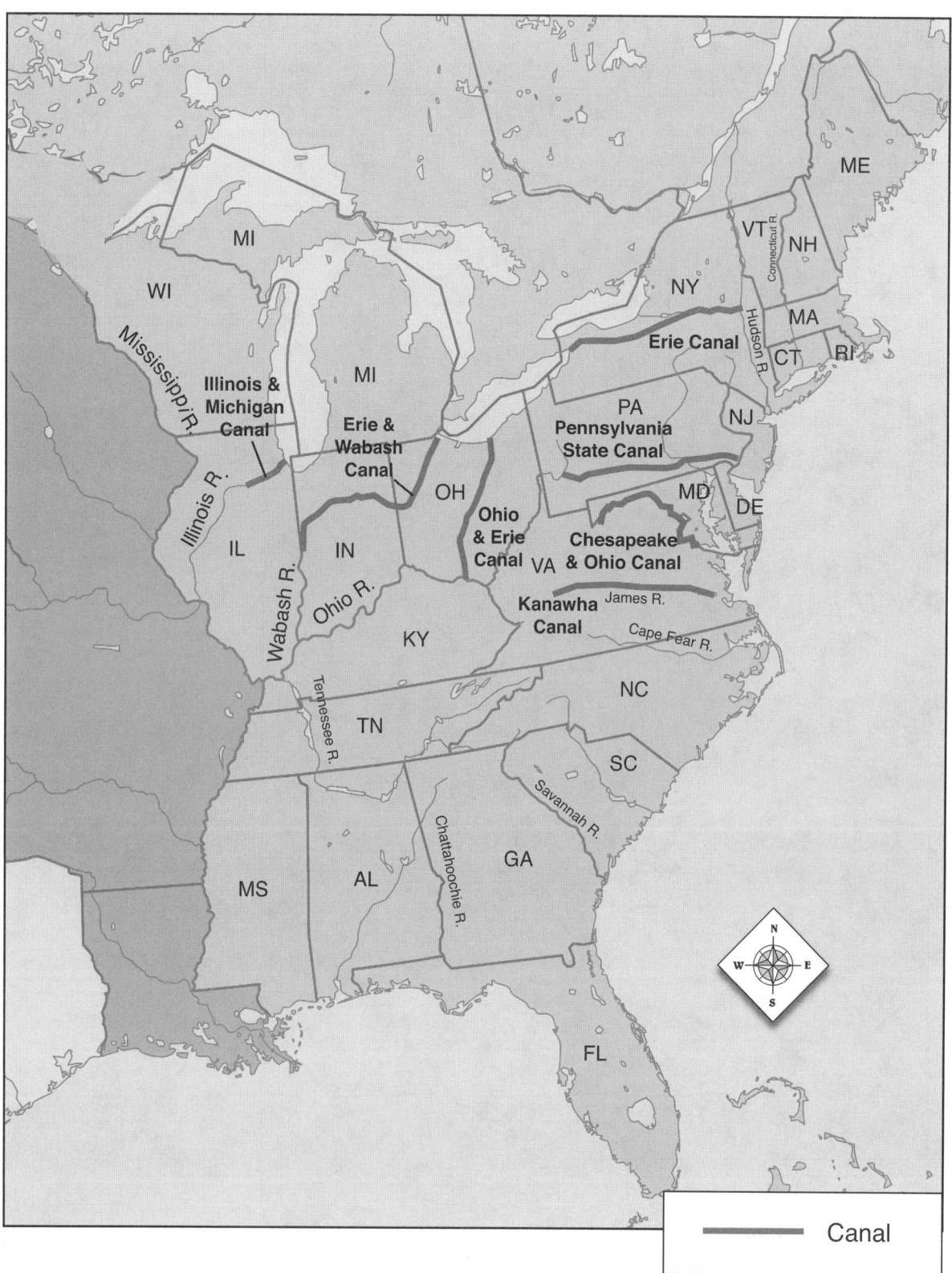

Name: _____
Date: _____

Texas War for Independence With Troop Movements and Battles

Maps for U.S. History

Texas War for Independence With Troop Movements and Battles

Map #: 045

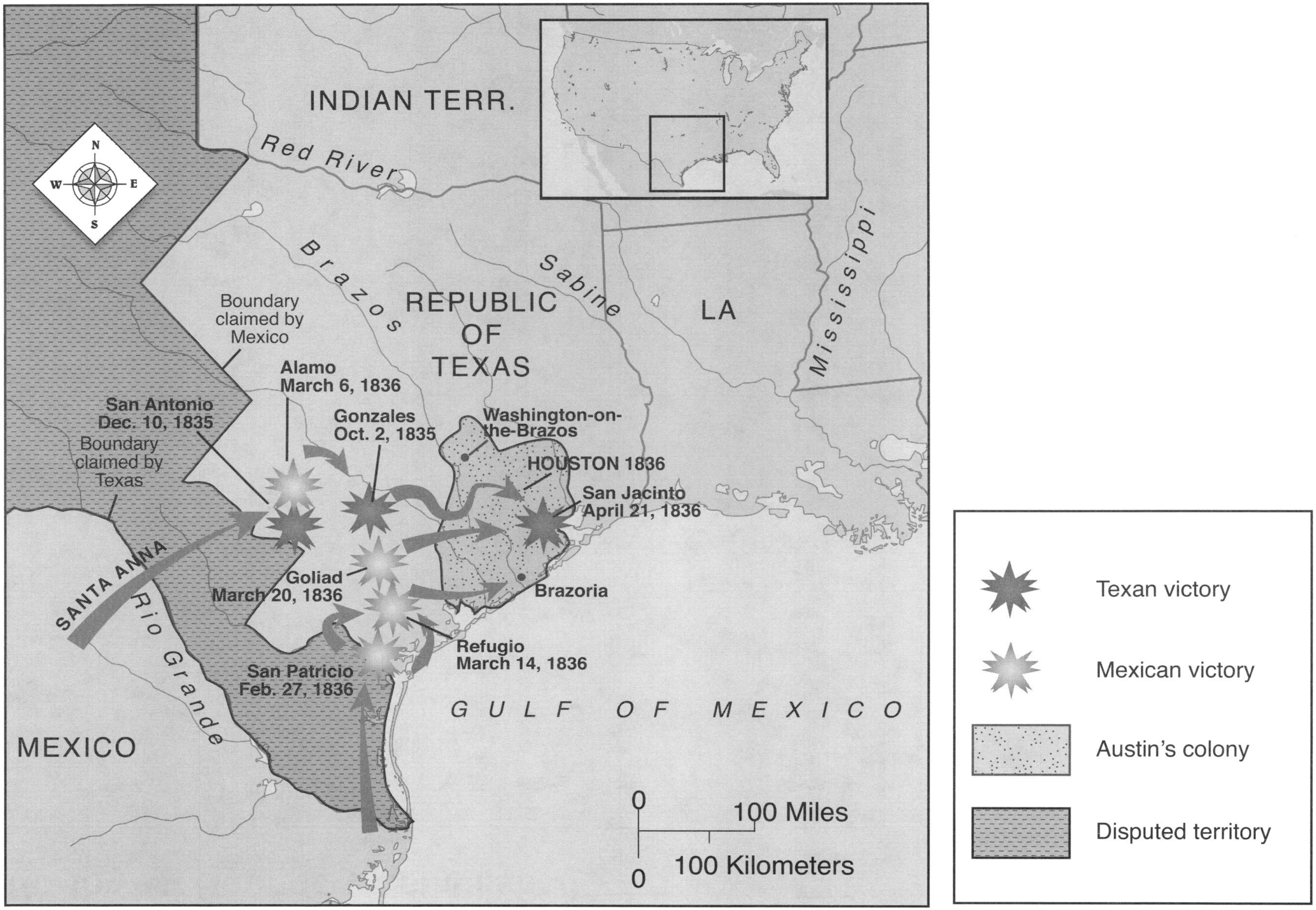

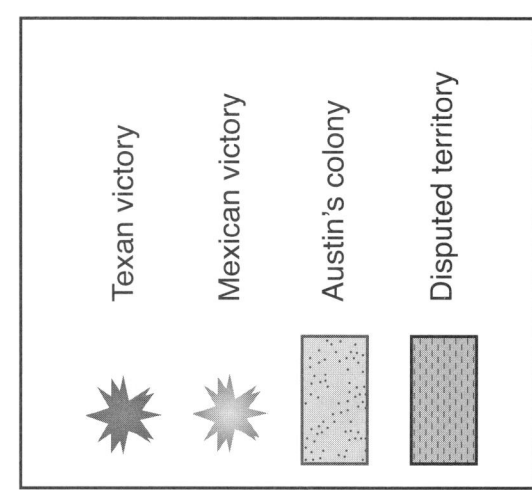

CD-405083 ©Mark Twain Media, Inc., Publishers

45

Name: _____   Date: _____

Northwest Boundary Established

Maps for U.S. History Northwest Boundary Established

Map #: 046

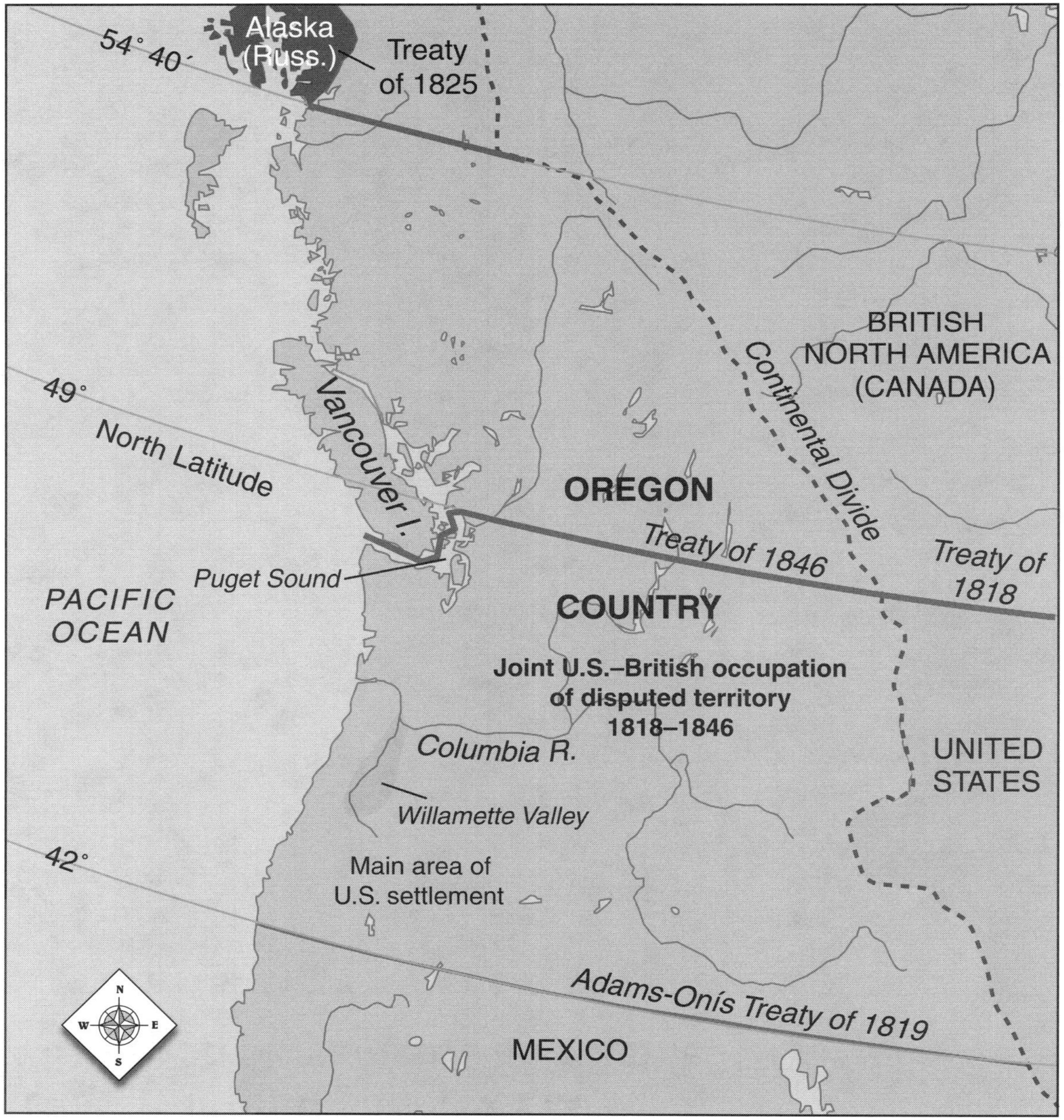

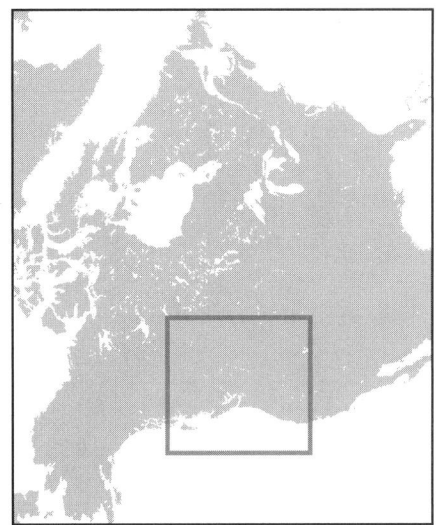

Name: _____ Date: _____

Oregon Country

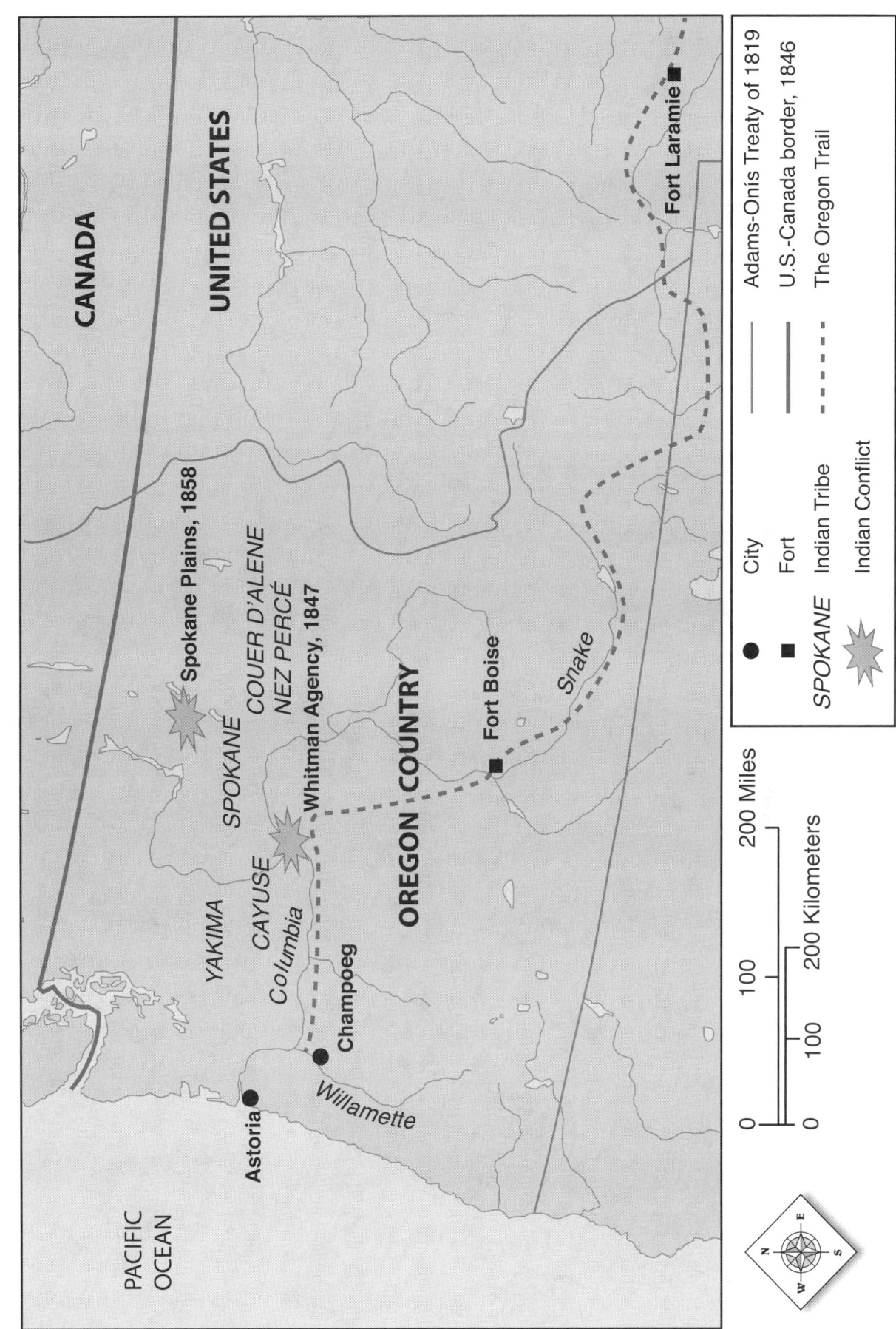

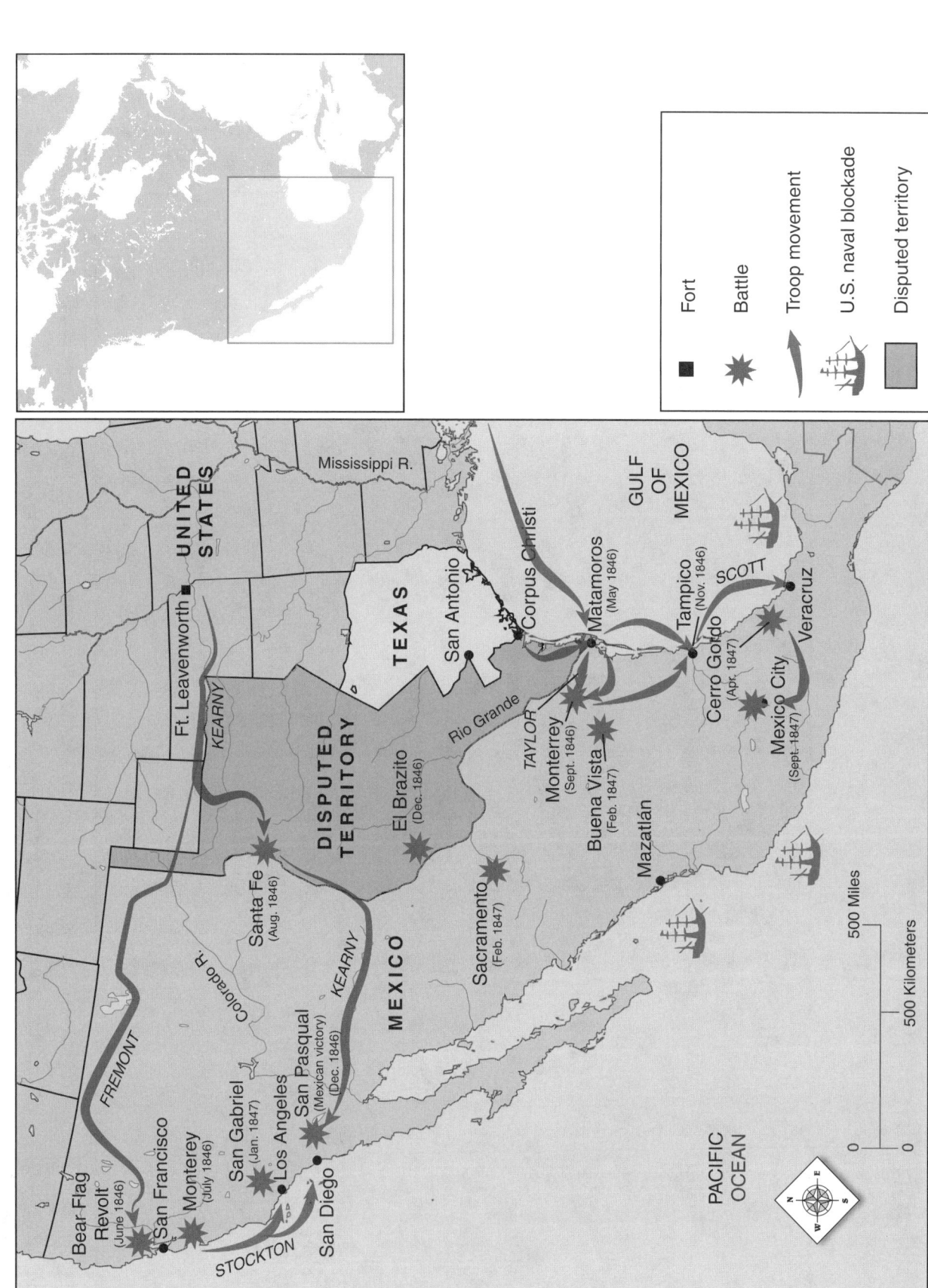

Name:
Date:

Major Gold Strikes in the California Gold Rush, 1848–1859

Maps for U.S. History — Major Gold Strikes in the California Gold Rush, 1848–1859

Map #: 049

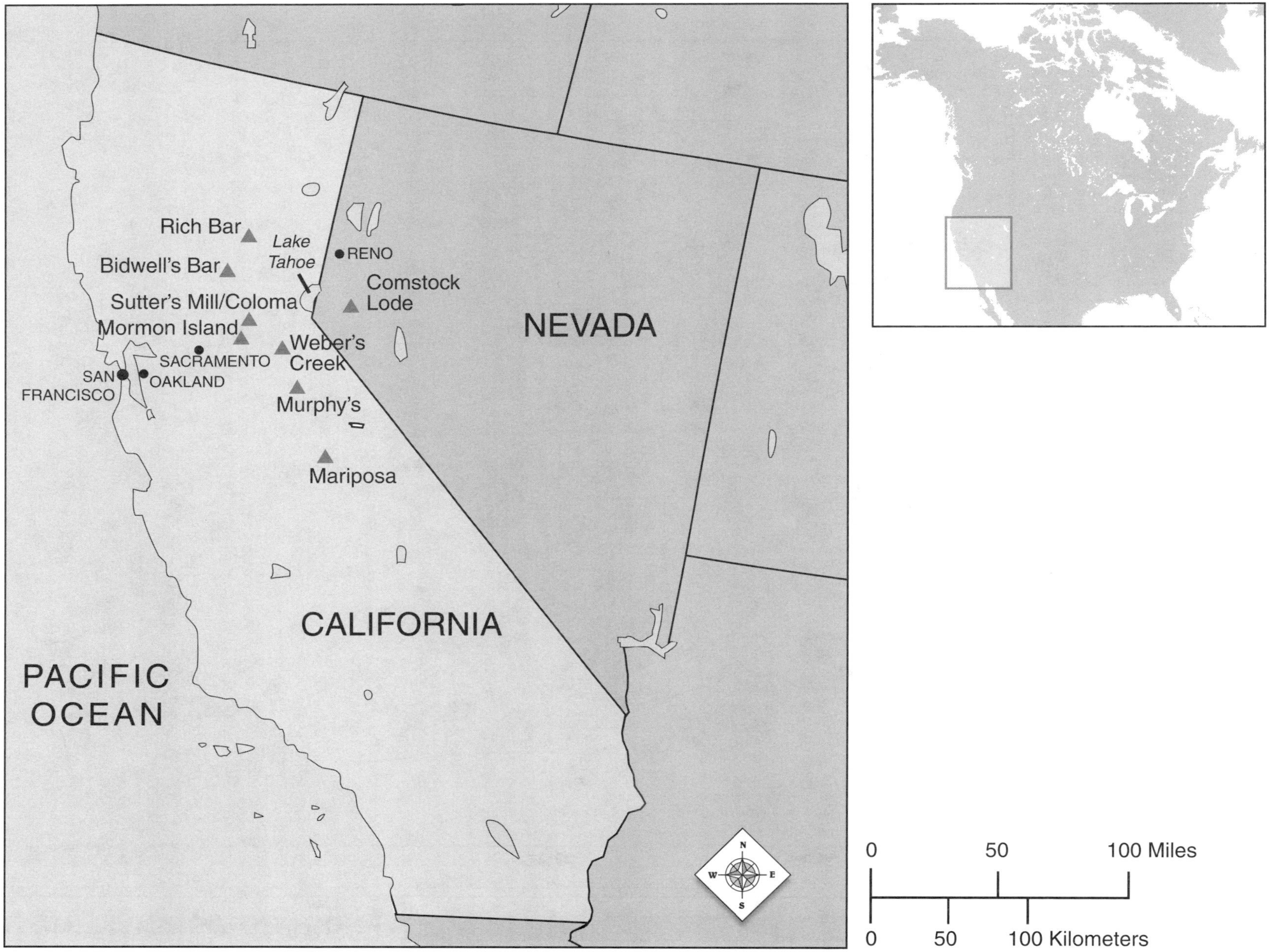

Locations shown on map:
- Rich Bar
- Bidwell's Bar
- Sutter's Mill/Coloma
- Mormon Island
- Lake Tahoe
- Weber's Creek
- Murphy's
- Mariposa
- Comstock Lode
- RENO
- SACRAMENTO
- OAKLAND
- SAN FRANCISCO

NEVADA
CALIFORNIA
PACIFIC OCEAN

Scale: 0–100 Miles / 0–100 Kilometers

CD-405083 ©Mark Twain Media, Inc., Publishers

Name: _____ Date: _____

Compromise of 1850

Maps for U.S. History Compromise of 1850

Map #: 050

Free states & territories
Slave states
Slavery determined by popular sovereignty

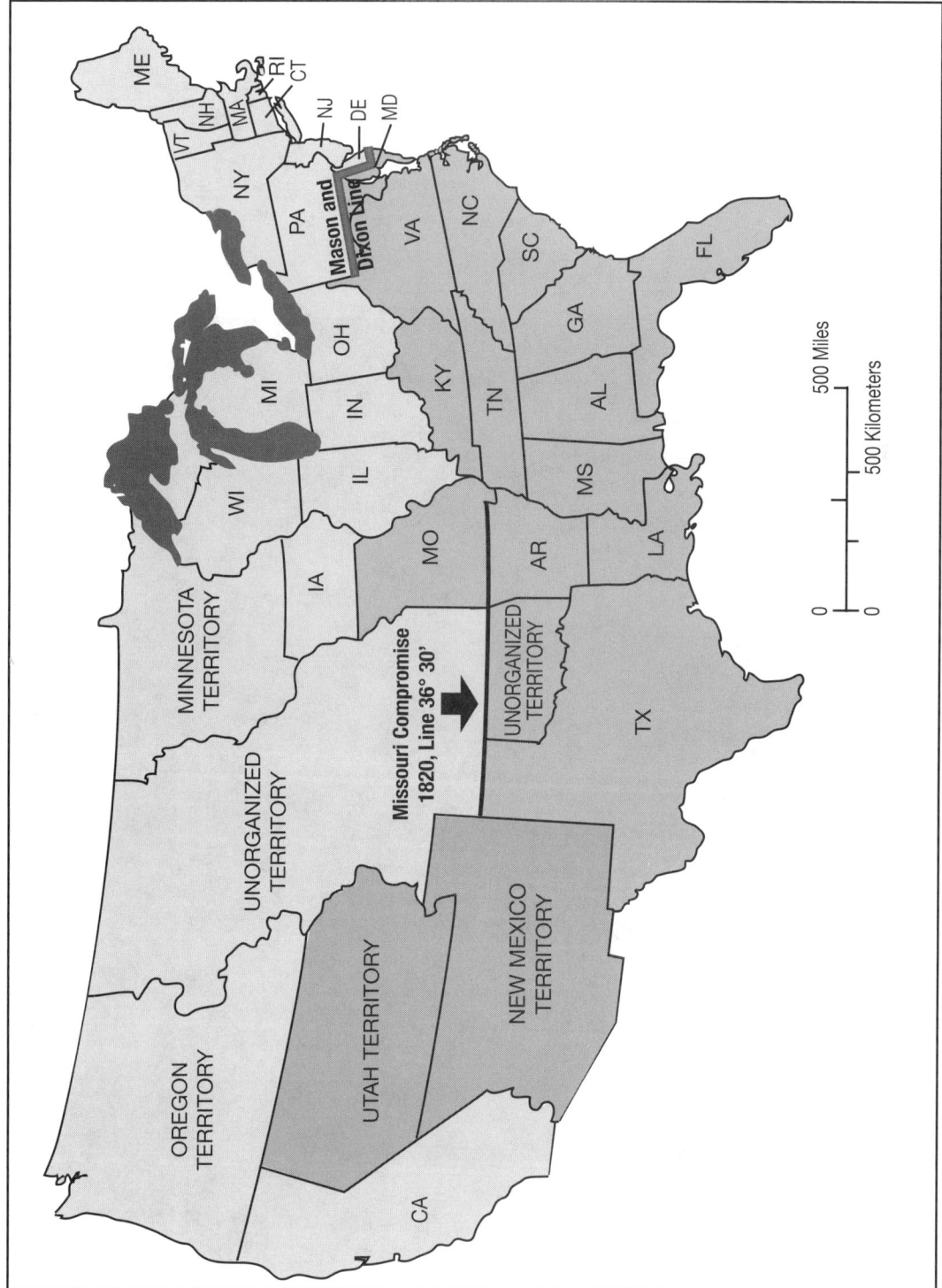

CD-405083 ©Mark Twain Media, Inc., Publishers   50

Name: _____ Date: _____

Kansas-Nebraska Act, 1854

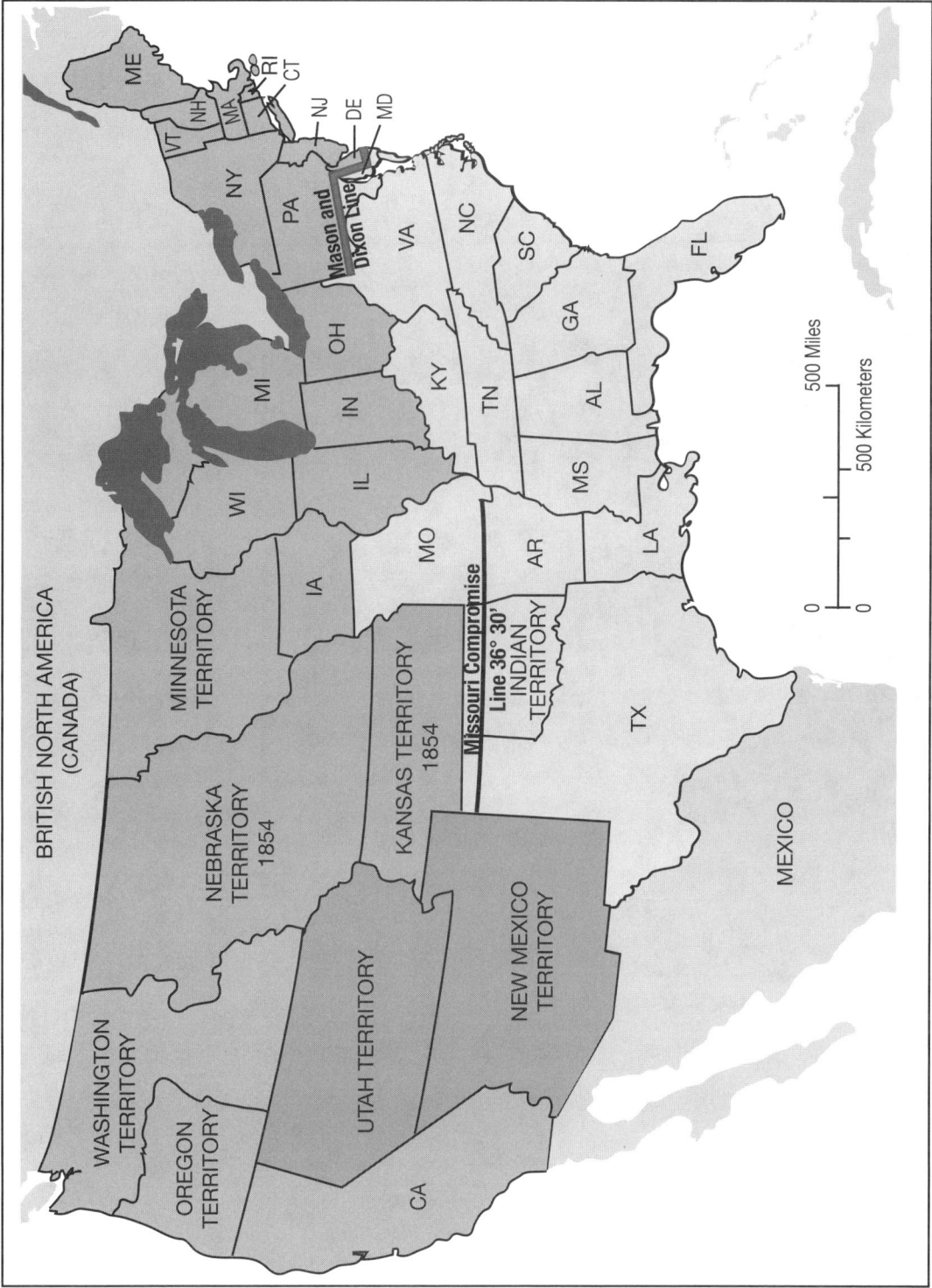

Name: ______________________ Date: ______________

Bleeding Kansas, 1854–1858

Map #: 052

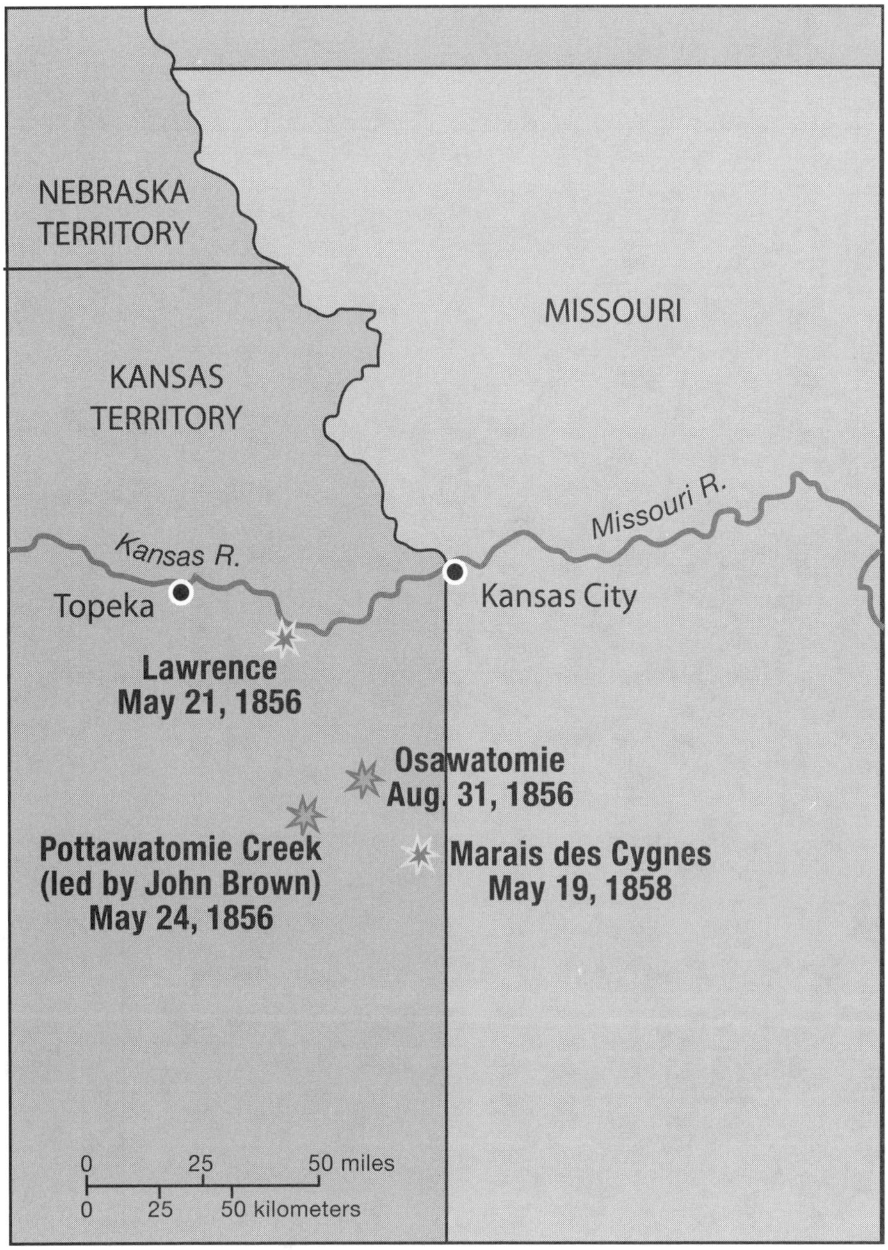

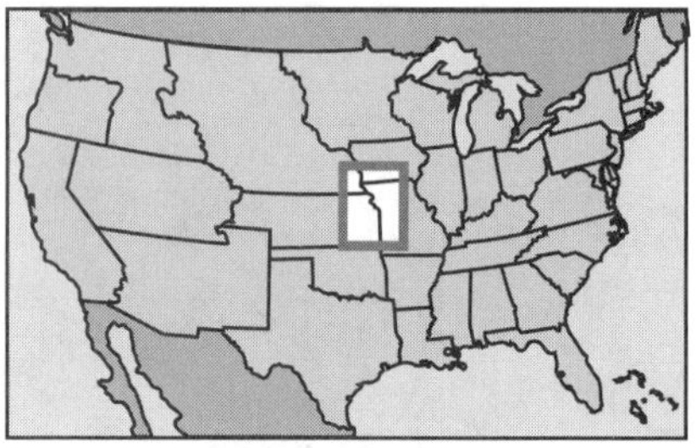

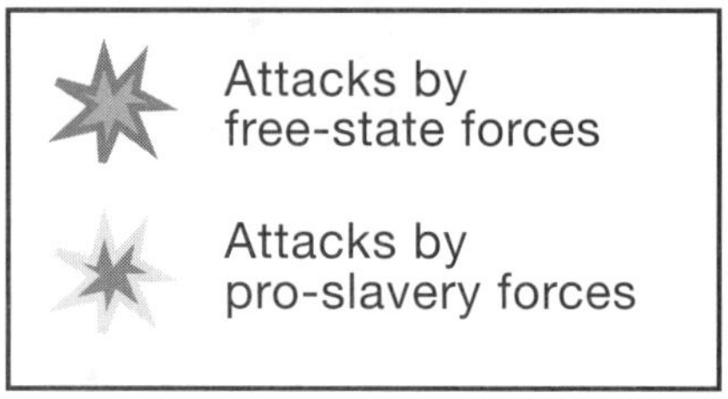

Name: _____ Date: _____

United States in 1856: Free States, Slave States, and Territories

Maps for U.S. History

United States in 1856: Free States, Slave States, and Territories

Map #: 053

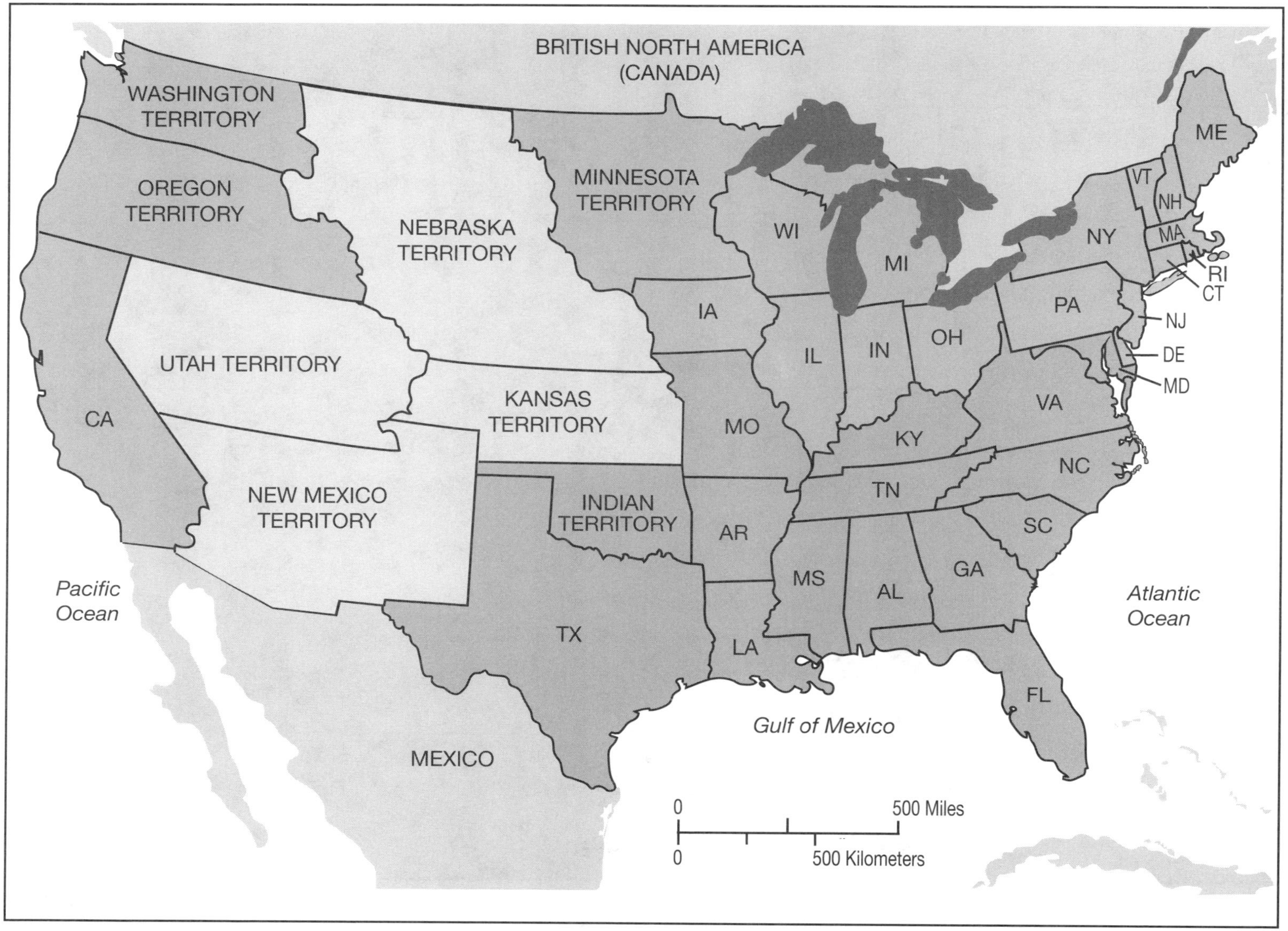

Legend:
- Free states and territories
- Slave states
- Territories open to slavery

Free States: ME, NH, VT, MA, RI, CT, NY, NJ, PA, OH, IN, IL, MI, WI, IA, CA

Slave States: DE, MD, VA, NC, SC, GA, FL, KY, TN, AL, MS, AR, LA, MO, TX

Territories open to slavery: Kansas Territory, New Mexico Territory, Utah Territory, Indian Territory

Free Territories: Washington Territory, Oregon Territory, Nebraska Territory, Minnesota Territory

BRITISH NORTH AMERICA (CANADA)

MEXICO

Atlantic Ocean

Gulf of Mexico

Pacific Ocean

500 Miles / 500 Kilometers

CD-405083 ©Mark Twain Media, Inc., Publishers

Name: _____ Date: _____

Pony Express Route

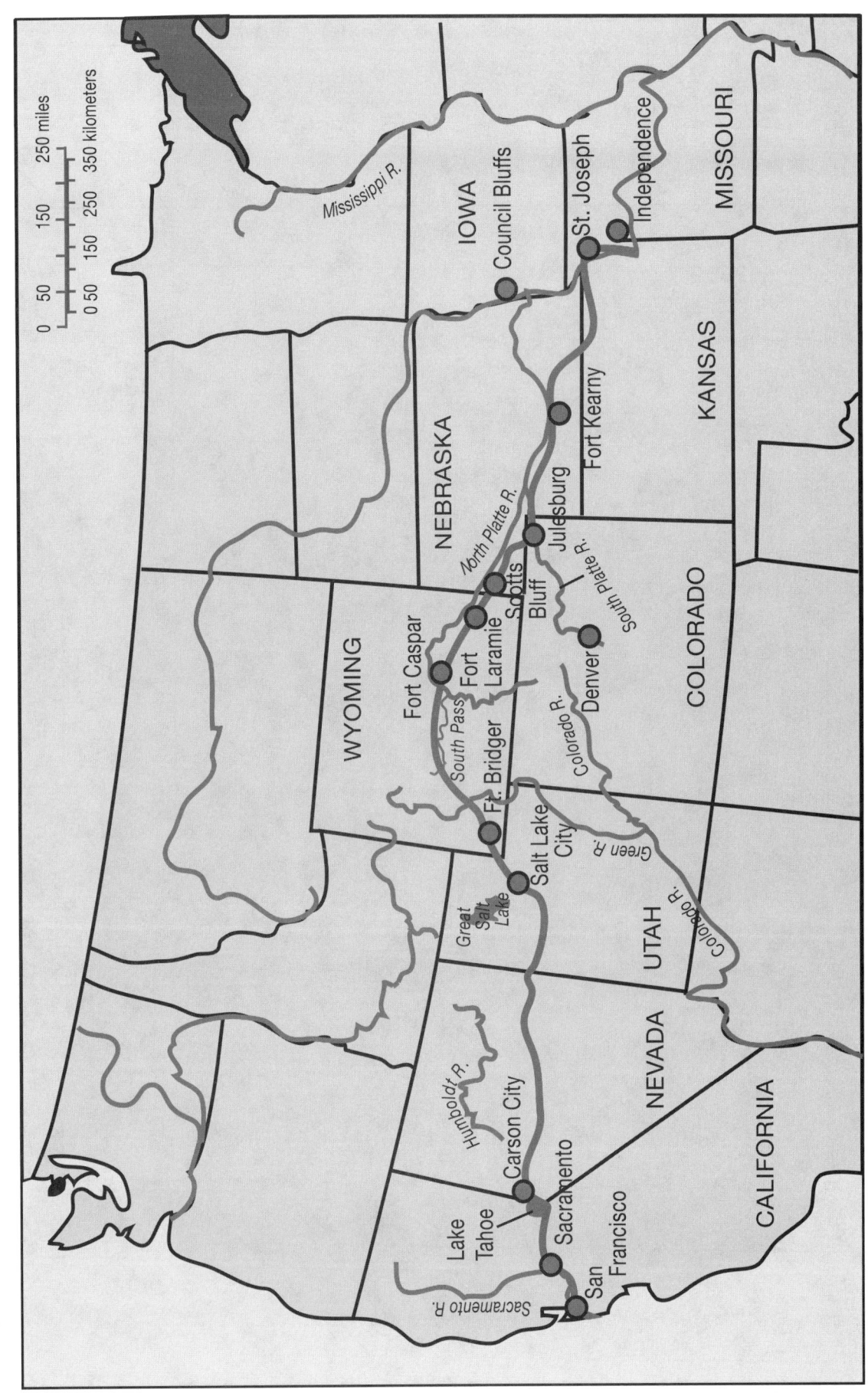

Name: ______________________________ Date: ____________________

The Underground Railroad

Map #: 055

Free states

Slave holding states

Territories

Major routes of escape

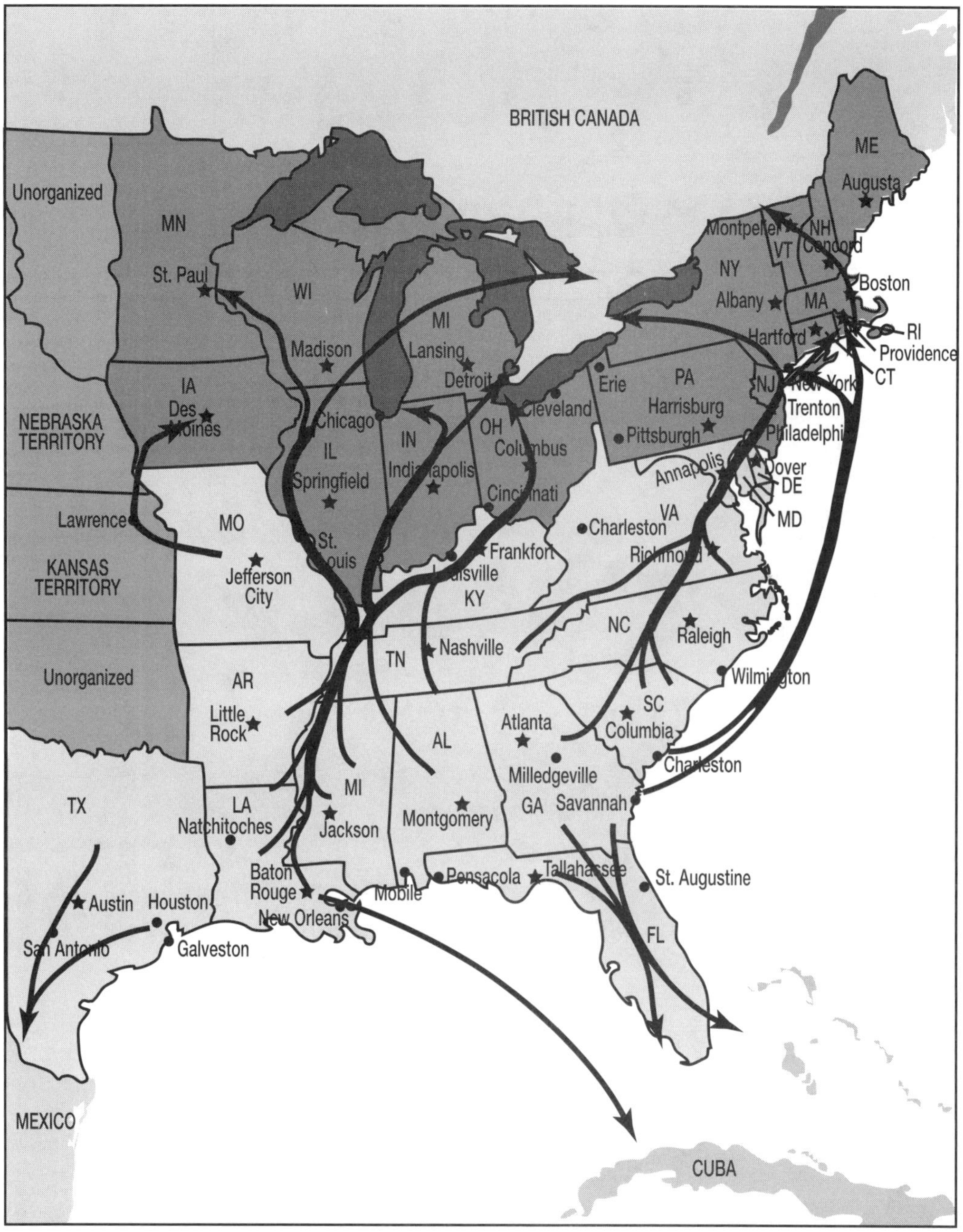

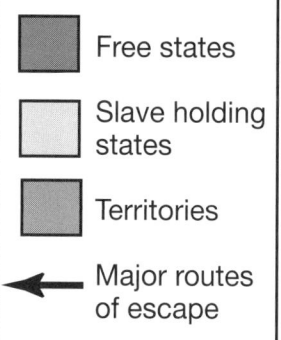

Name: ______________________ Date: ______________________

Resources of the Northern and Southern States Before 1860

Map #: 056

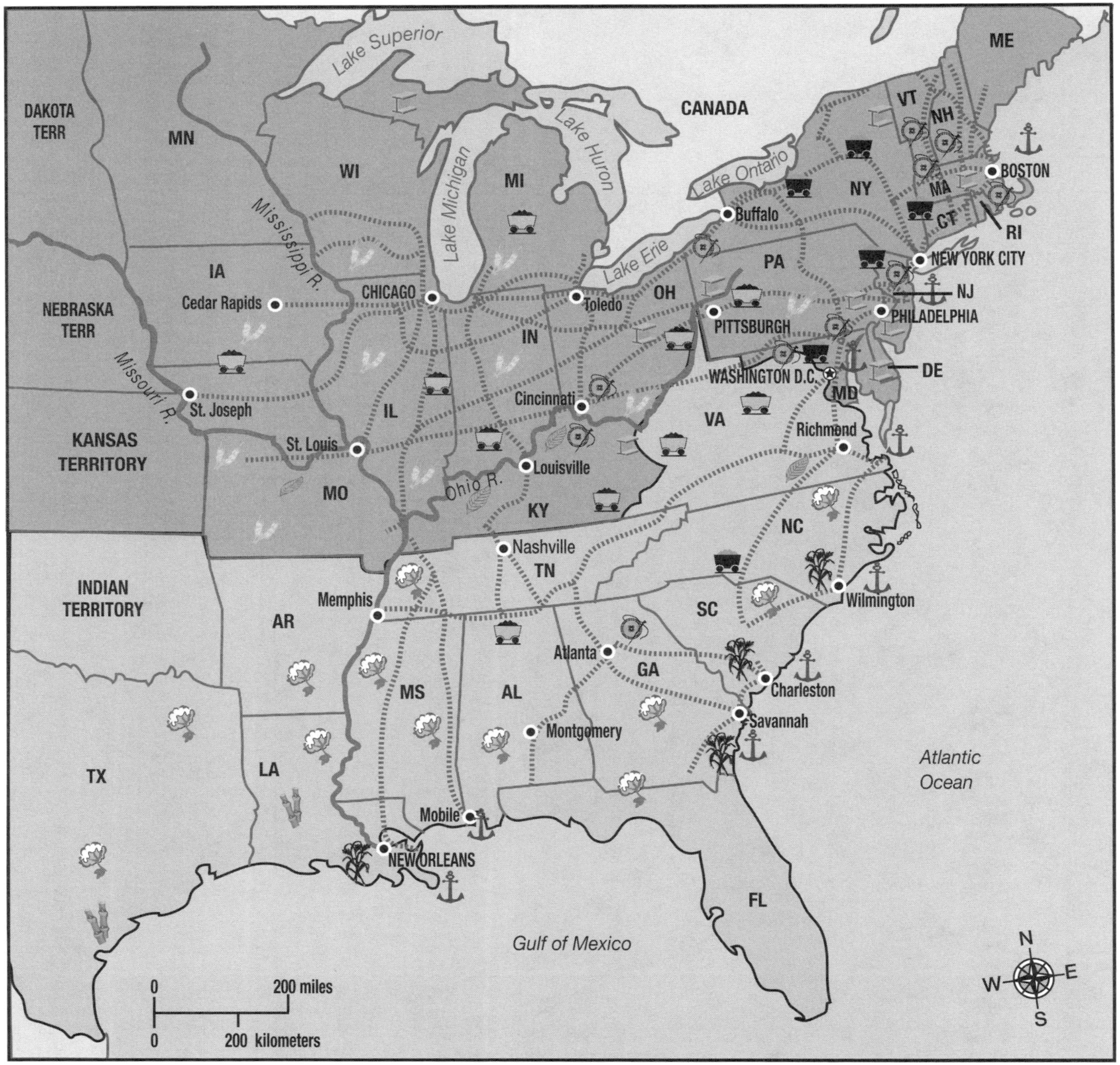

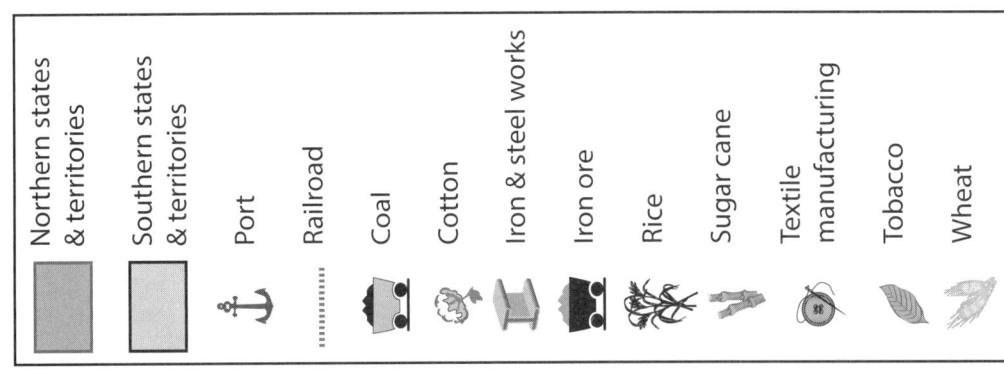

Maps for U.S. History — Population Density of Enslaved Persons, 1860

Map #: 057

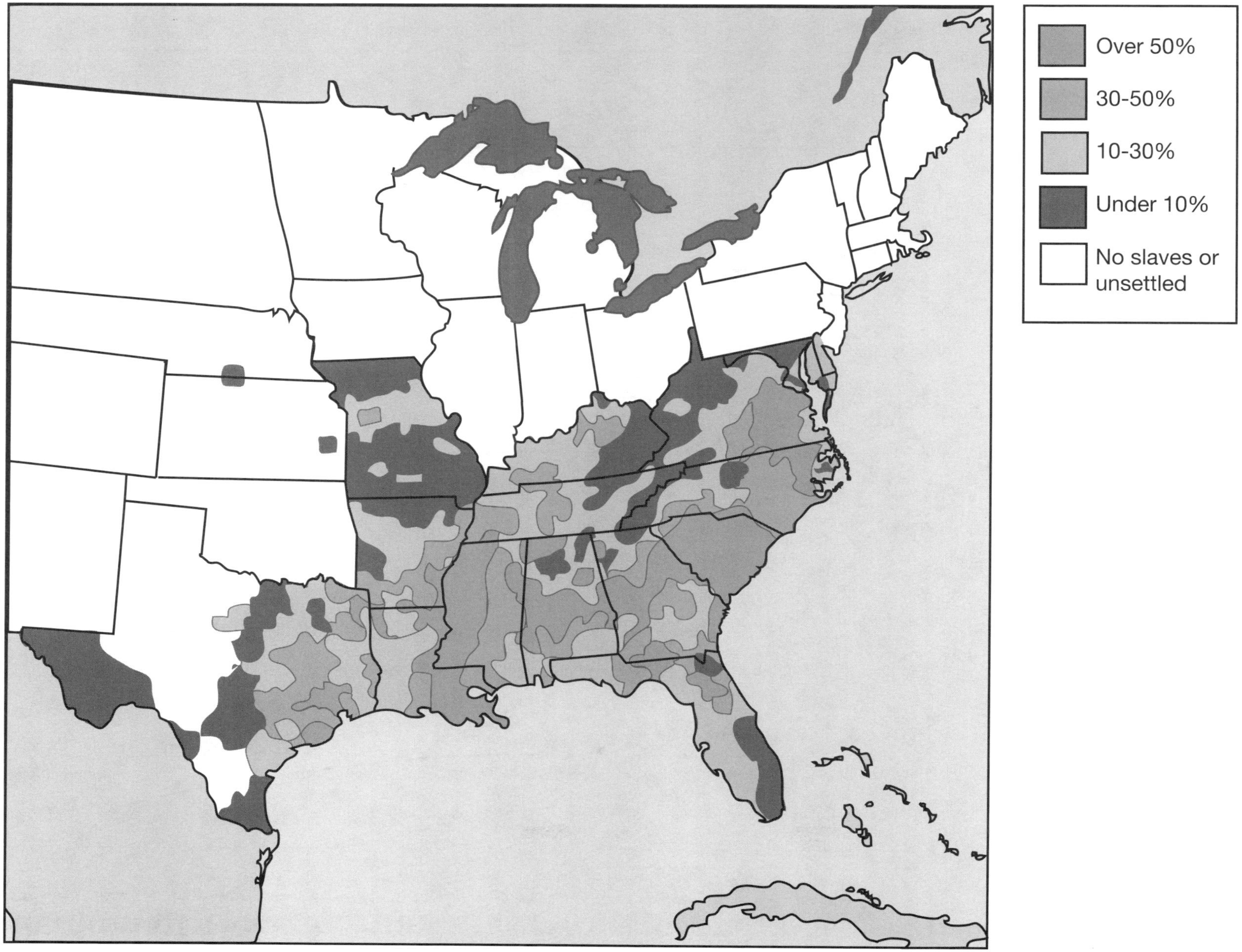

Name: _____ Date: _____

Population Density of Enslaved Persons, 1860

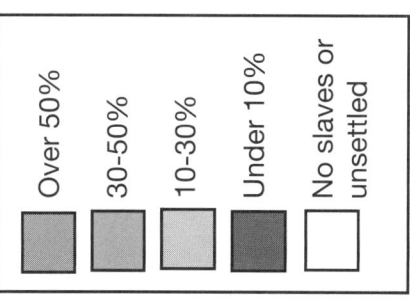

Legend:
- Over 50%
- 30–50%
- 10–30%
- Under 10%
- No slaves or unsettled

Name: _____ Date: _____

Election of 1860

Maps for U.S. History — Election of 1860

Map #: 058

Legend:
- Lincoln (Republican)
- Bell (Constitutional Union)
- Douglas (Northern Democratic)
- Breckinridge (Southern Democratic)
- Non-voting Territories

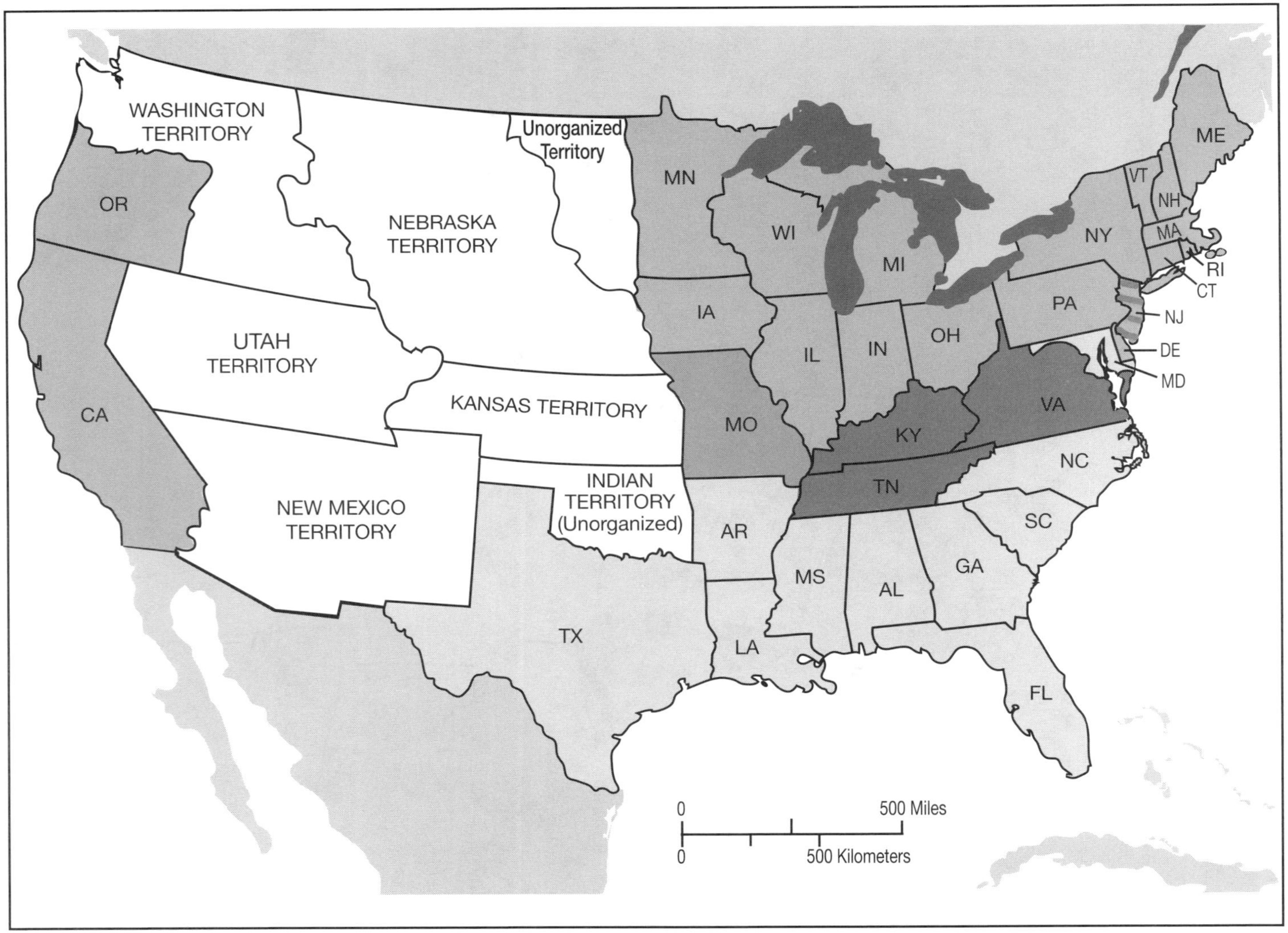

Name: _____

Date: _____

Railroads Prior to the Civil War

Maps for U.S. History　　　　　　　　　　　　　　　　　　　Railroads Prior to the Civil War

Map #: 059

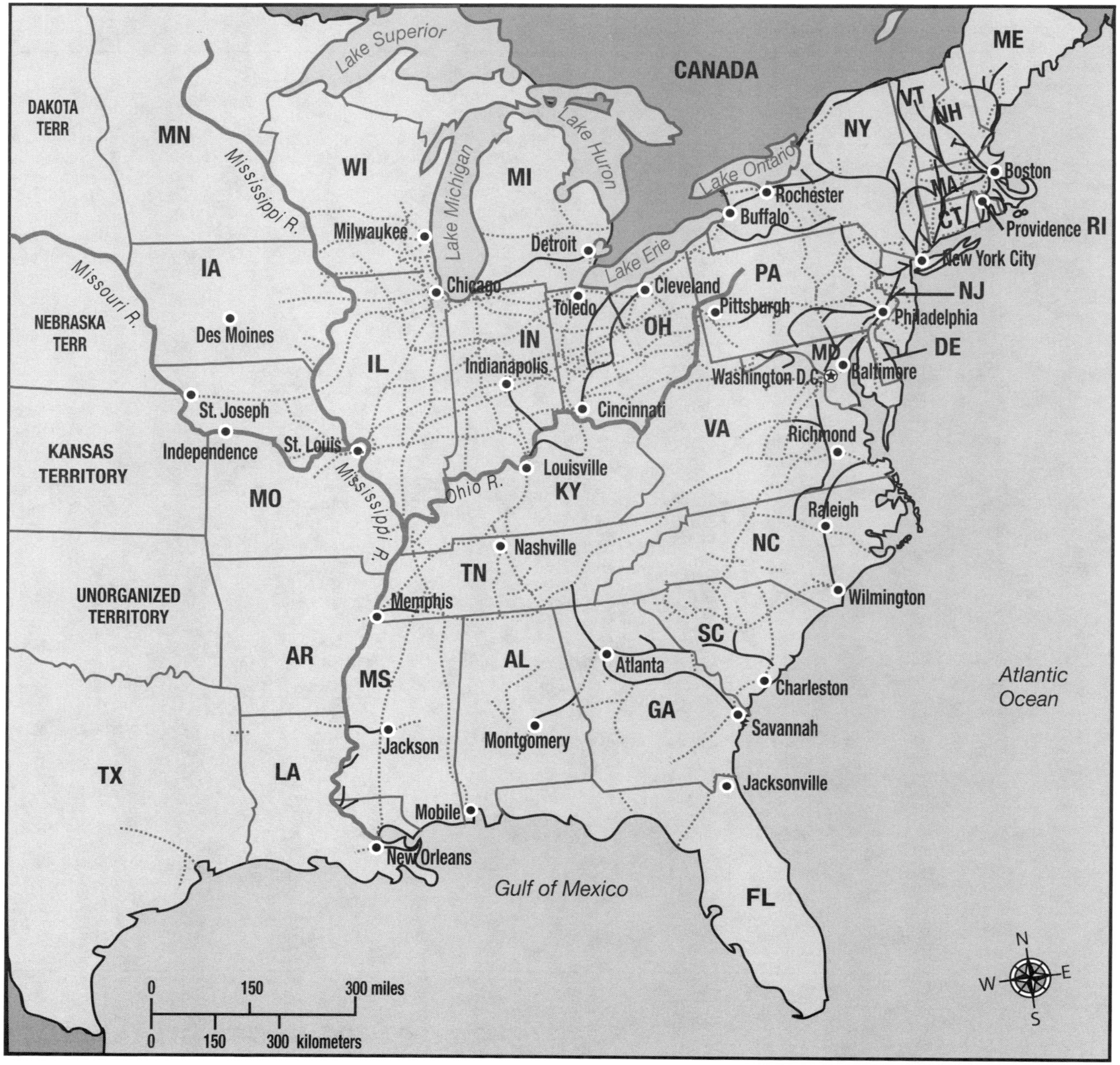

Legend:
- ········· Railroads in operation, 1850
- ———— Railroads added by 1861

Name: _____ Date: _____

Union and Confederate States

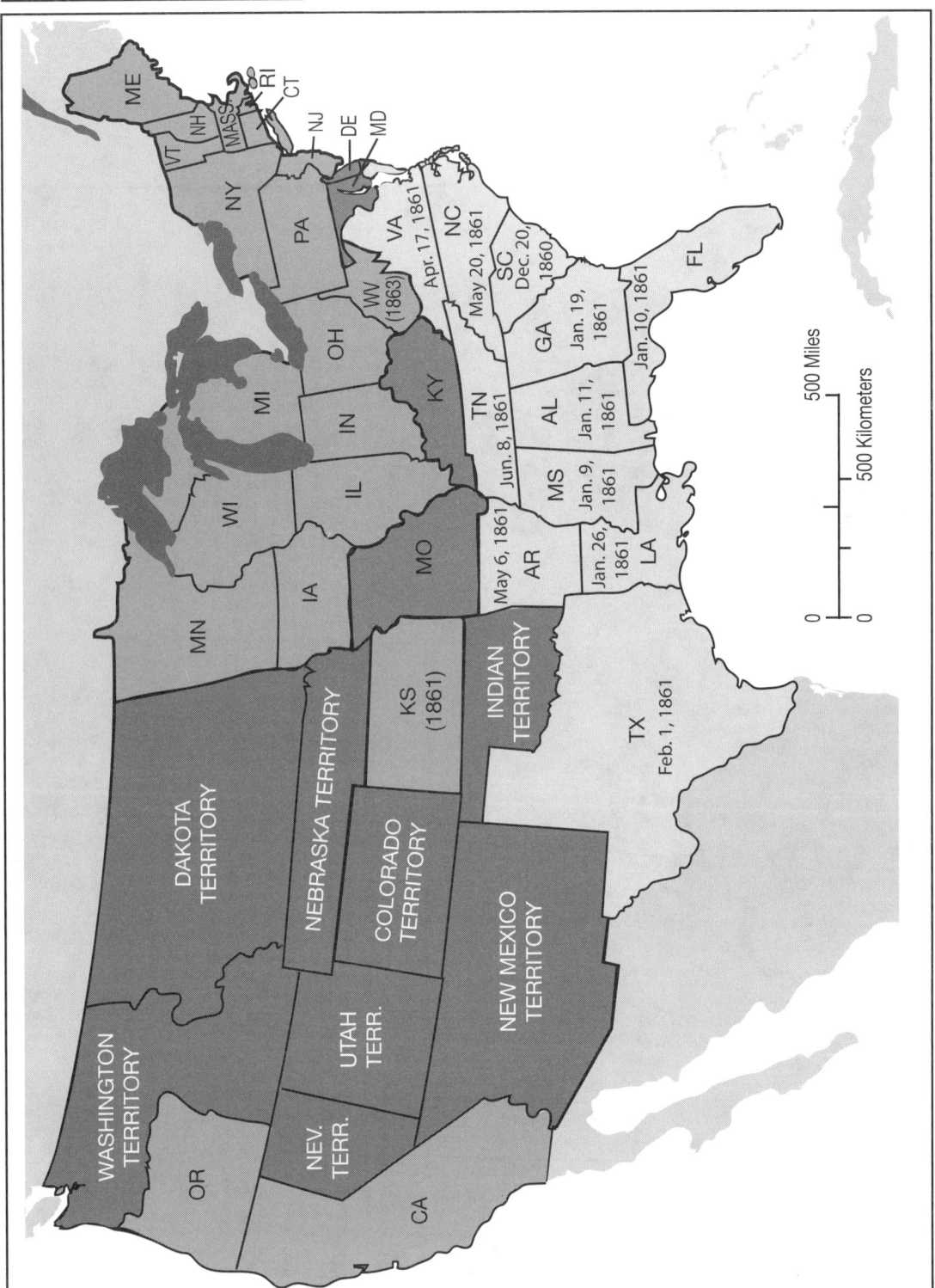

Maps for U.S. History — Union and Confederate States

Map #: 060

Legend:
- Union states
- Confederate states
- Union territories
- Border states
- Dec. 20, 1860 — Date of secession from Union

Civil War Strategy

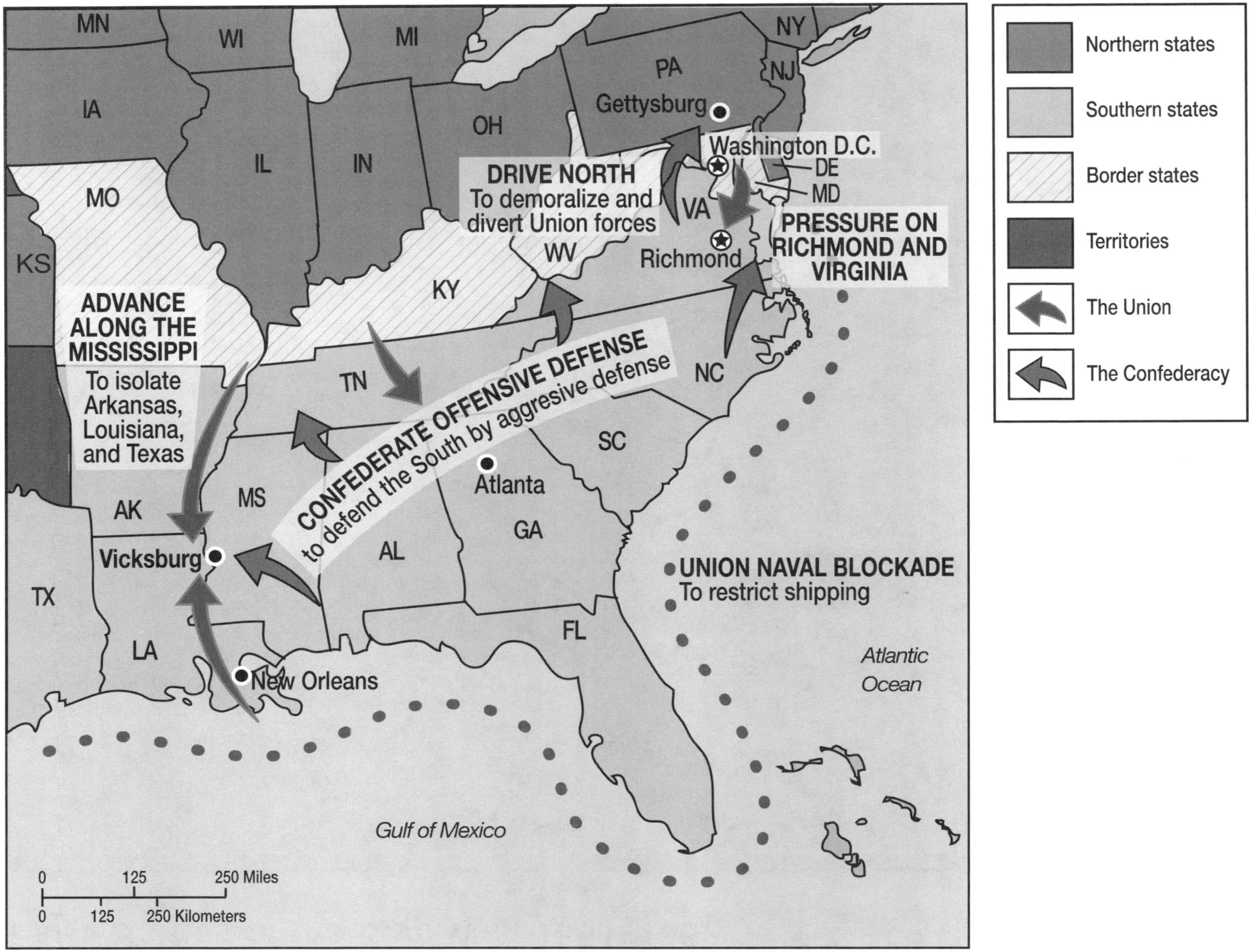

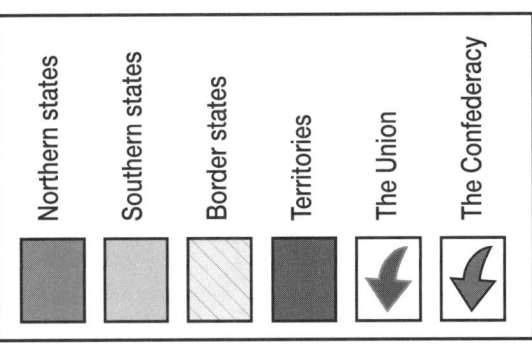

Name: _____ Date: _____

Early Battles of the Civil War, 1861–1862

Map #: 062

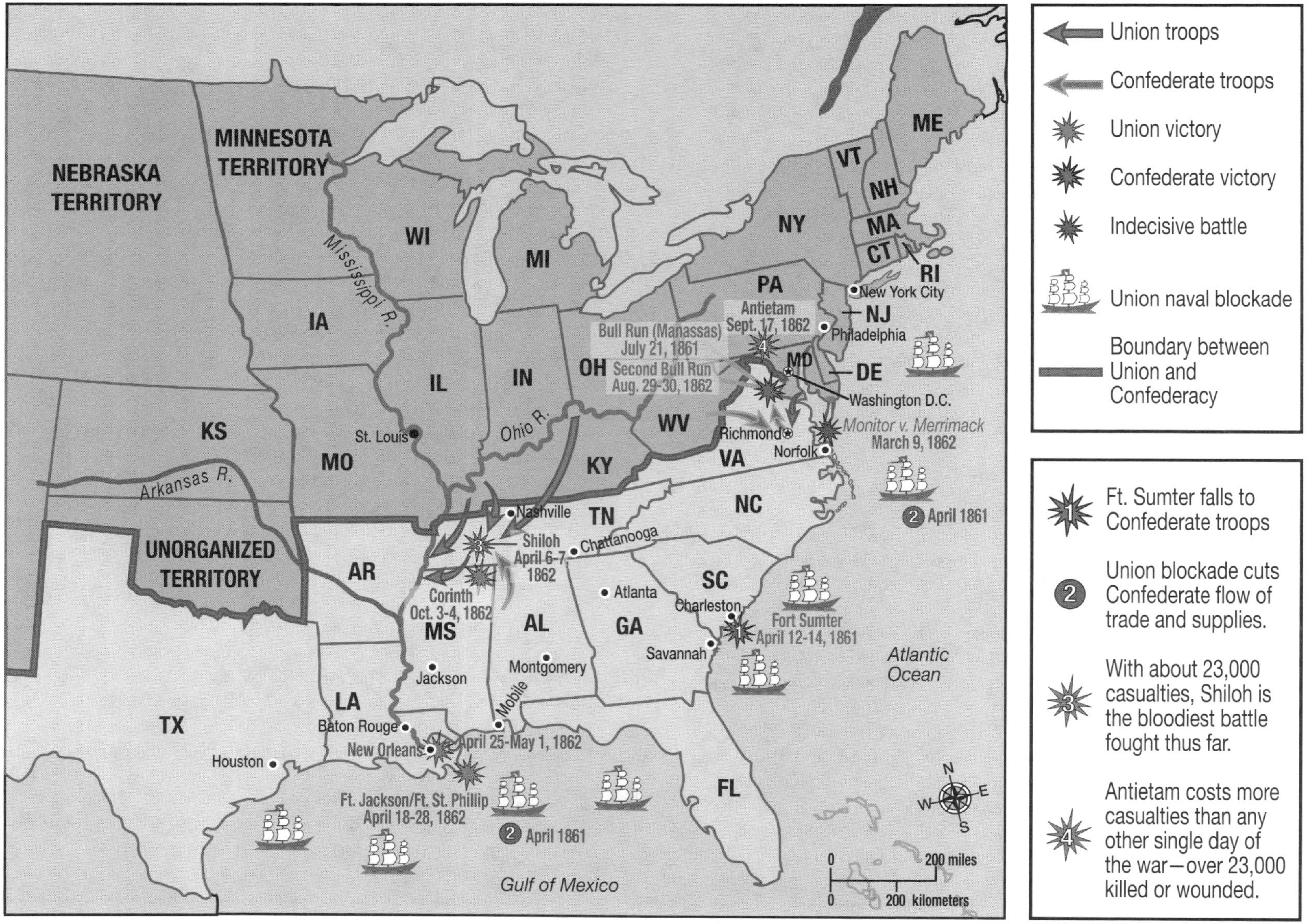

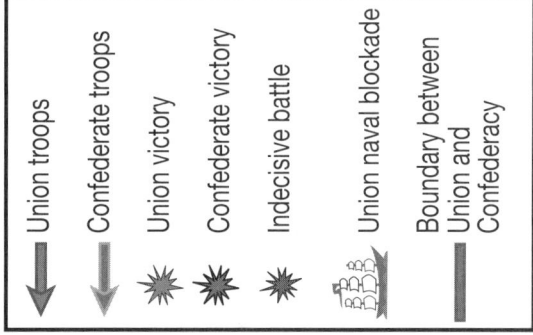
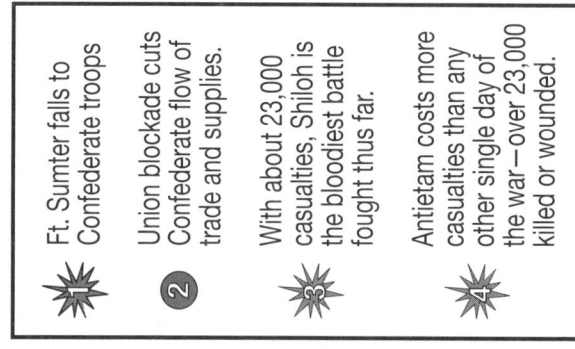

Name: _____   Date: _____

Civil War Battles, 1862–1863

Map #: 063

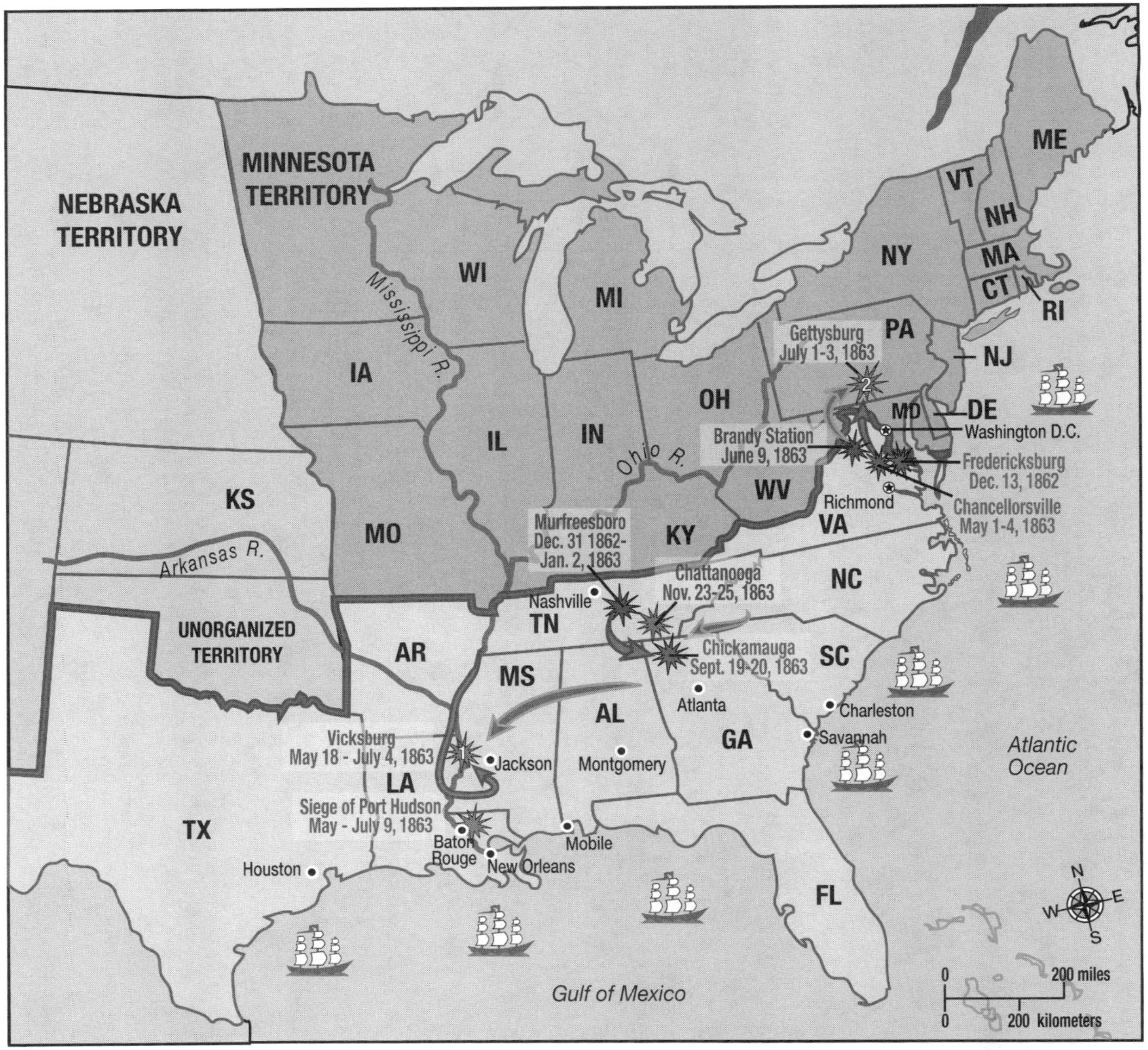

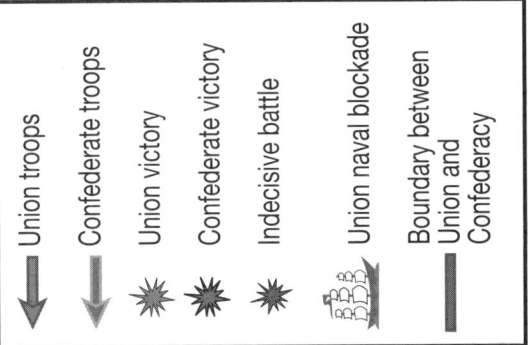

Legend:
- Union troops
- Confederate troops
- Union victory
- Confederate victory
- Indecisive battle
- Union naval blockade
- Boundary between Union and Confederacy

Union victories at Vicksburg & Gettysburg marked the turning point of the Civil War.

1. Siege of Vicksburg ends with a Confederate surrender; Union isolates western Confederacy.

2. After Gettysburg, southern troops never again penetrate so deeply into Union territory.

Maps for U.S. History

Battle of Gettysburg

Name: _____ Date: _____

Battle of Gettysburg

Map #: 064

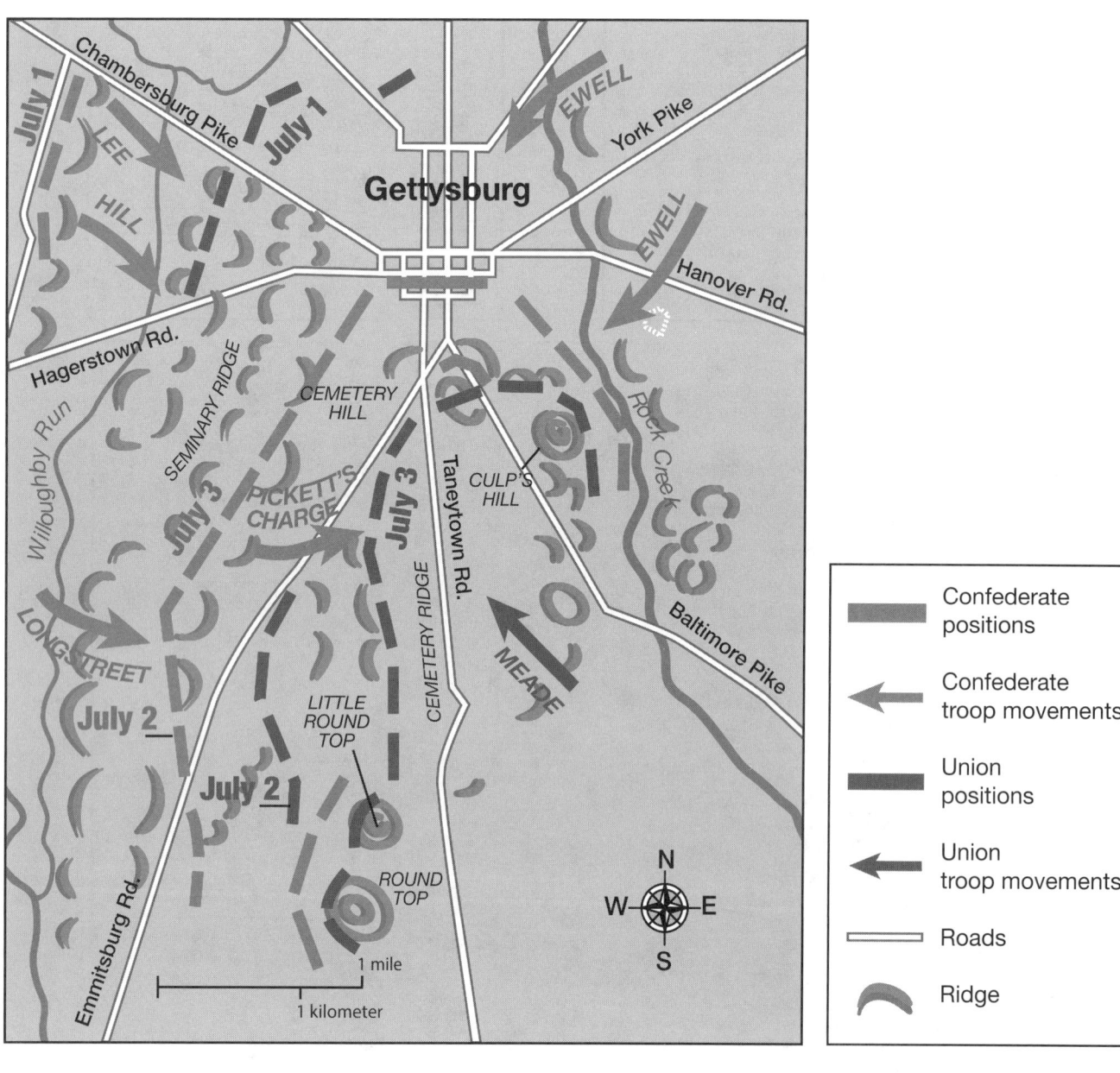

Name: _____ Date: _____

Final Civil War Battles, 1864–1865

Maps for U.S. History
Final Civil War Battles, 1864–1865

Map #: 065

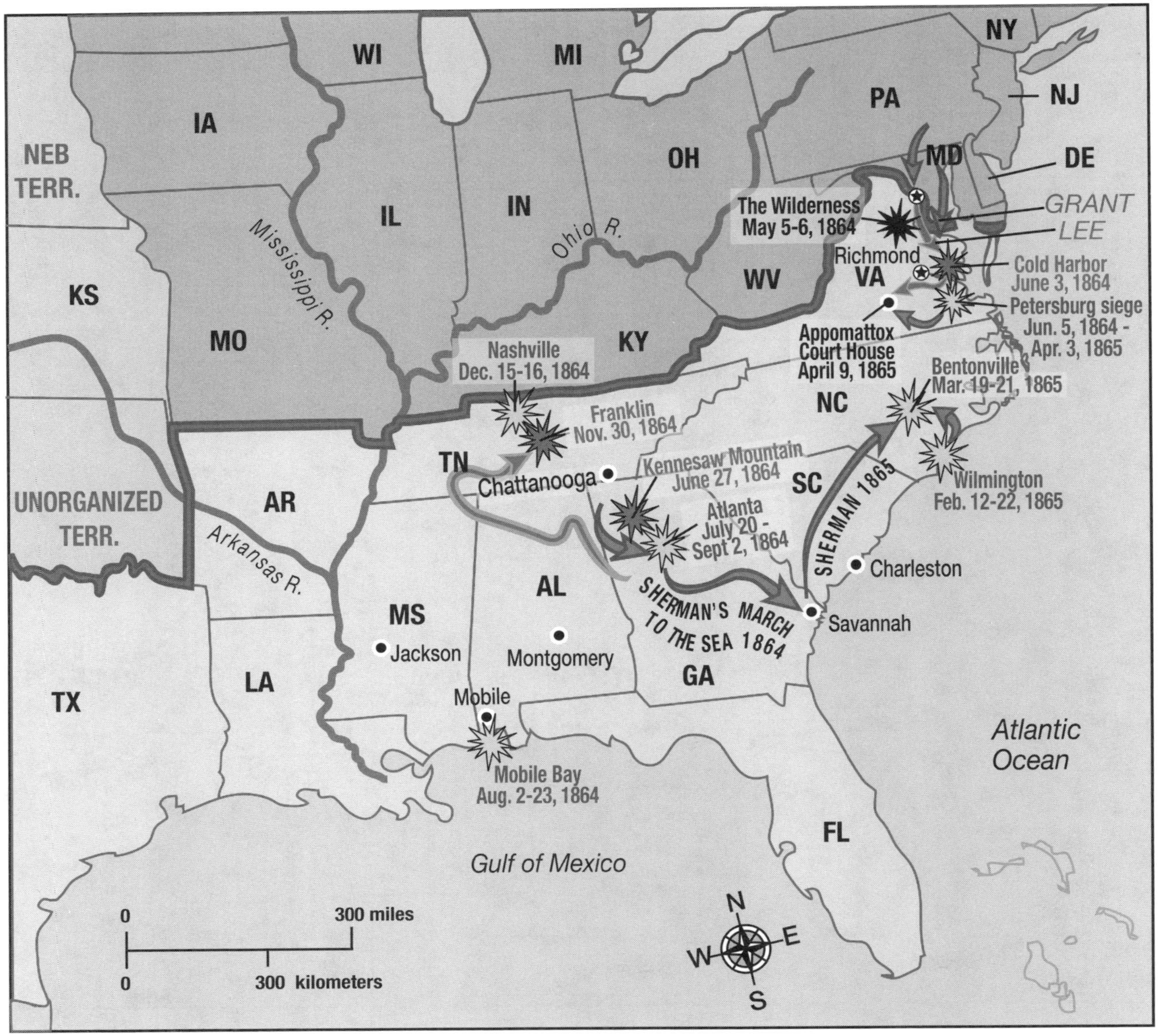

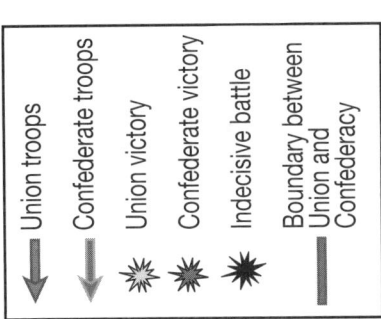

- Union troops
- Confederate troops
- Union victory
- Confederate victory
- Indecisive battle
- Boundary between Union and Confederacy

Reconstruction: Dates of Readmission to the Union and Reestablished Conservative Governments

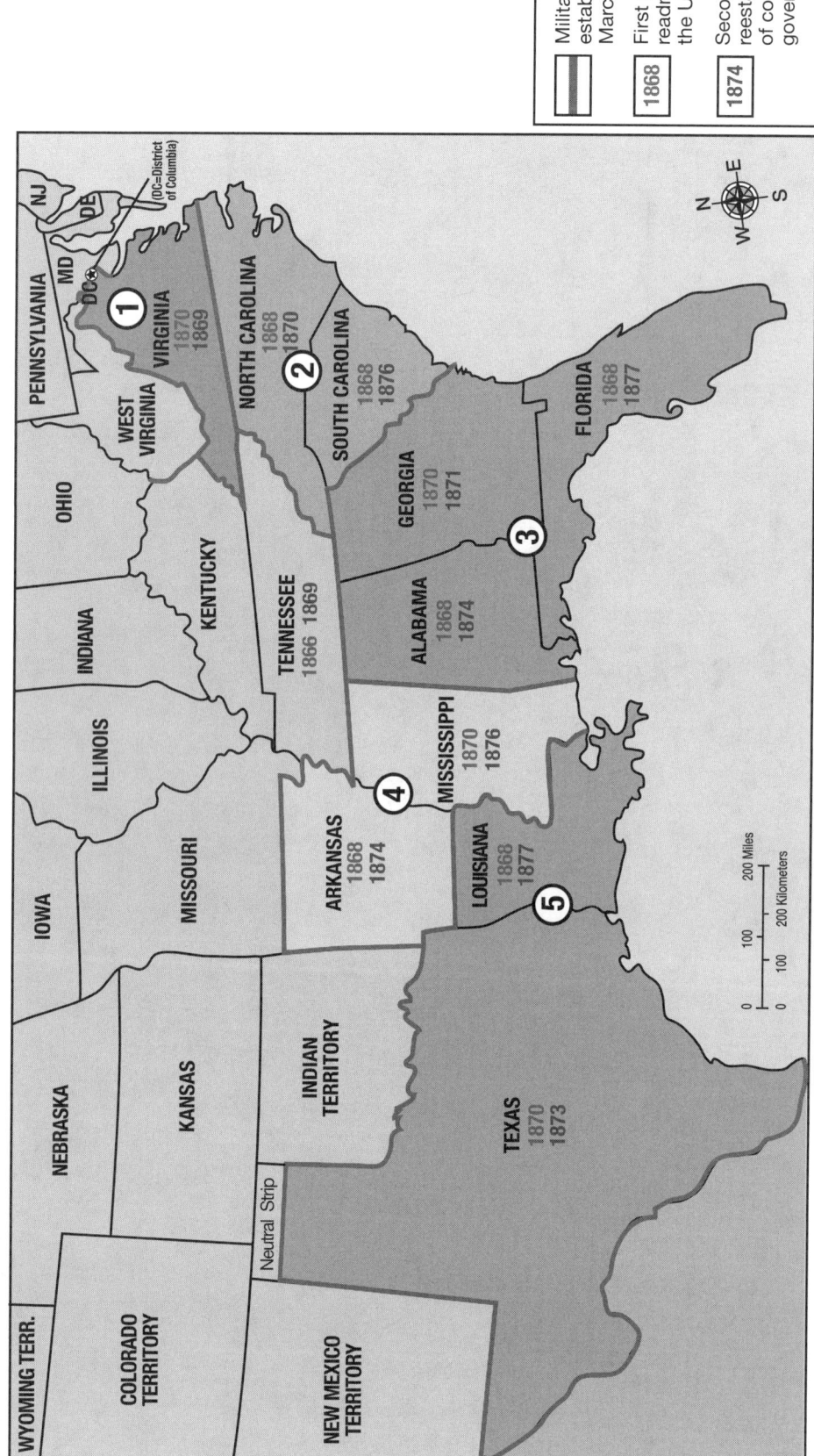

Name: _____ Date: _____

Major Battles With Native Americans, 1860–1890

Maps for U.S. History

Major Battles With Native Americans, 1860–1890

Map #: 067

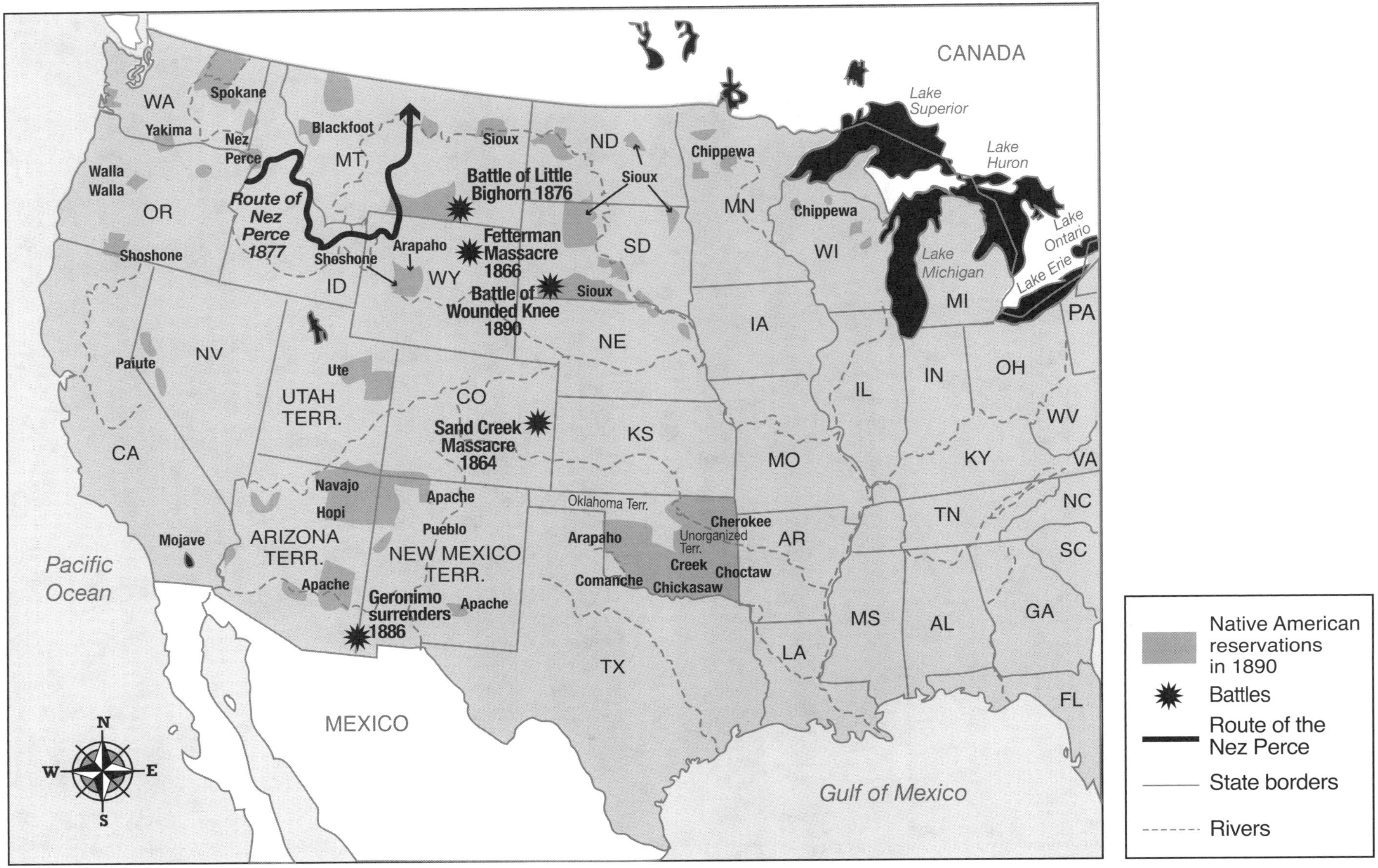

Legend:
- Native American reservations in 1890
- Battles
- Route of the Nez Perce
- State borders
- Rivers

Battles labeled on map:
- Battle of Little Bighorn 1876
- Fetterman Massacre 1866
- Battle of Wounded Knee 1890
- Sand Creek Massacre 1864
- Geronimo surrenders 1886
- Route of Nez Perce 1877

Tribes/Reservations labeled:
Chippewa, Sioux, Arapaho, Blackfoot, Shoshone, Spokane, Yakima, Nez Perce, Walla Walla, Shoshone, Paiute, Ute, Navajo, Hopi, Mojave, Apache, Pueblo, Arapaho, Comanche, Cherokee, Creek, Choctaw, Chickasaw

CD-405083 ©Mark Twain Media, Inc., Publishers

Name: _____ Date: _____

The Chisholm and Other Cattle Trails of the Western United States

Maps for U.S. History — The Chisholm and Other Cattle Trails of the Western United States

Map #: 068

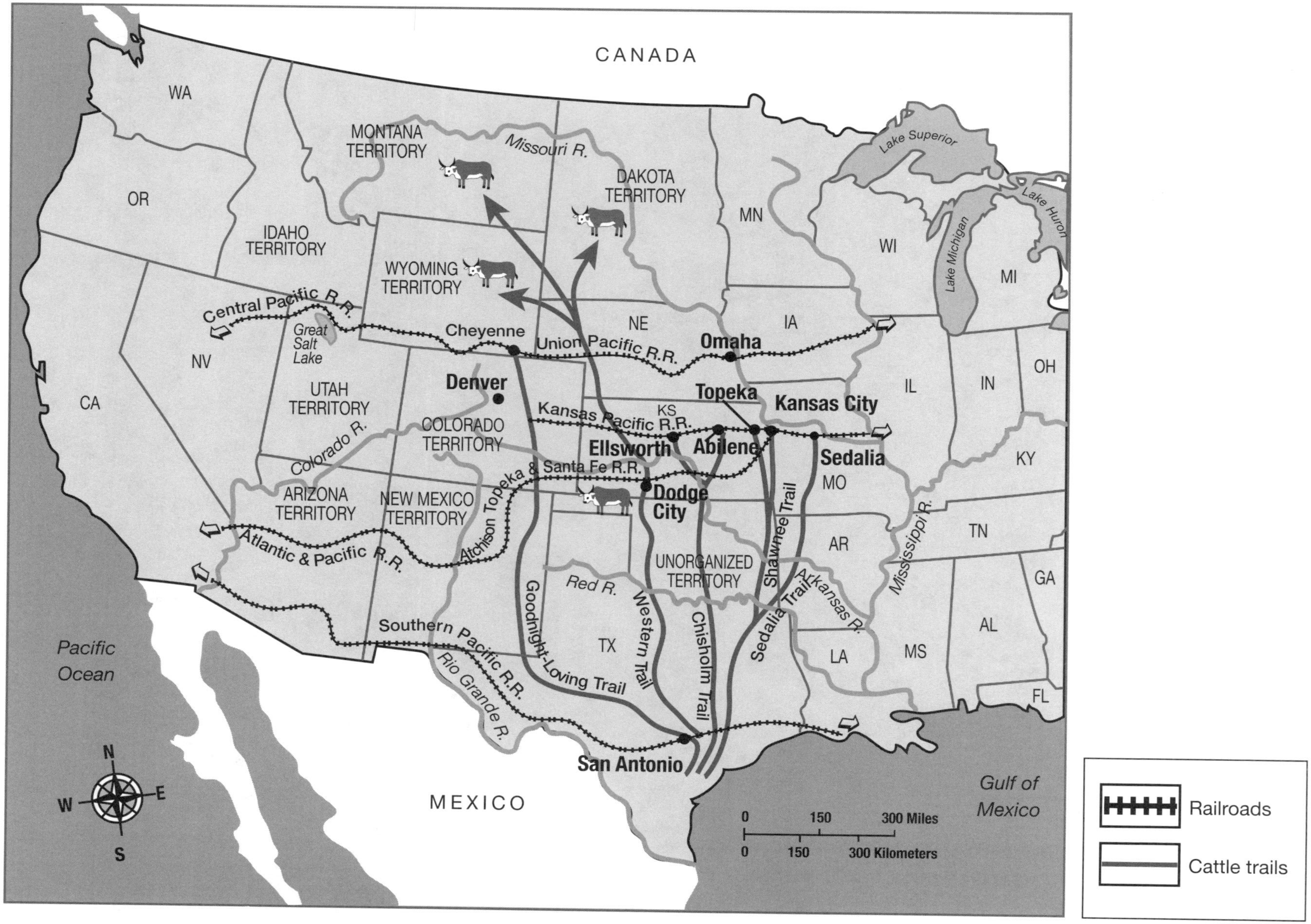

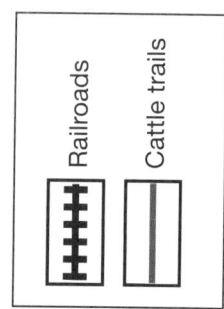
Railroads
Cattle trails

Name: _____ Date: _____

Maps for U.S. History
Map #: 069

States and Territories of the United States, 1868–1876

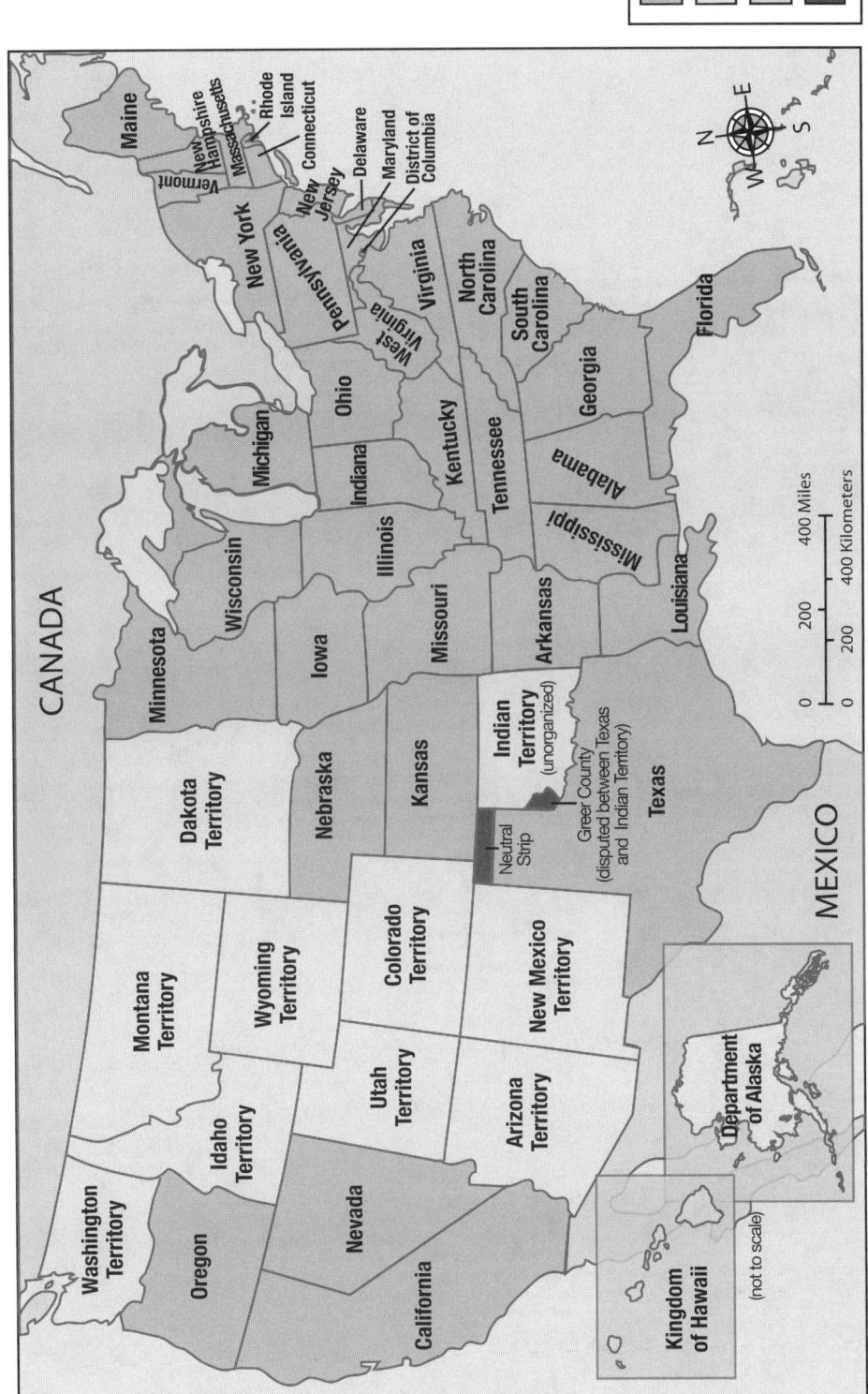

Name: _____ Date: _____

Transcontinental Railroad

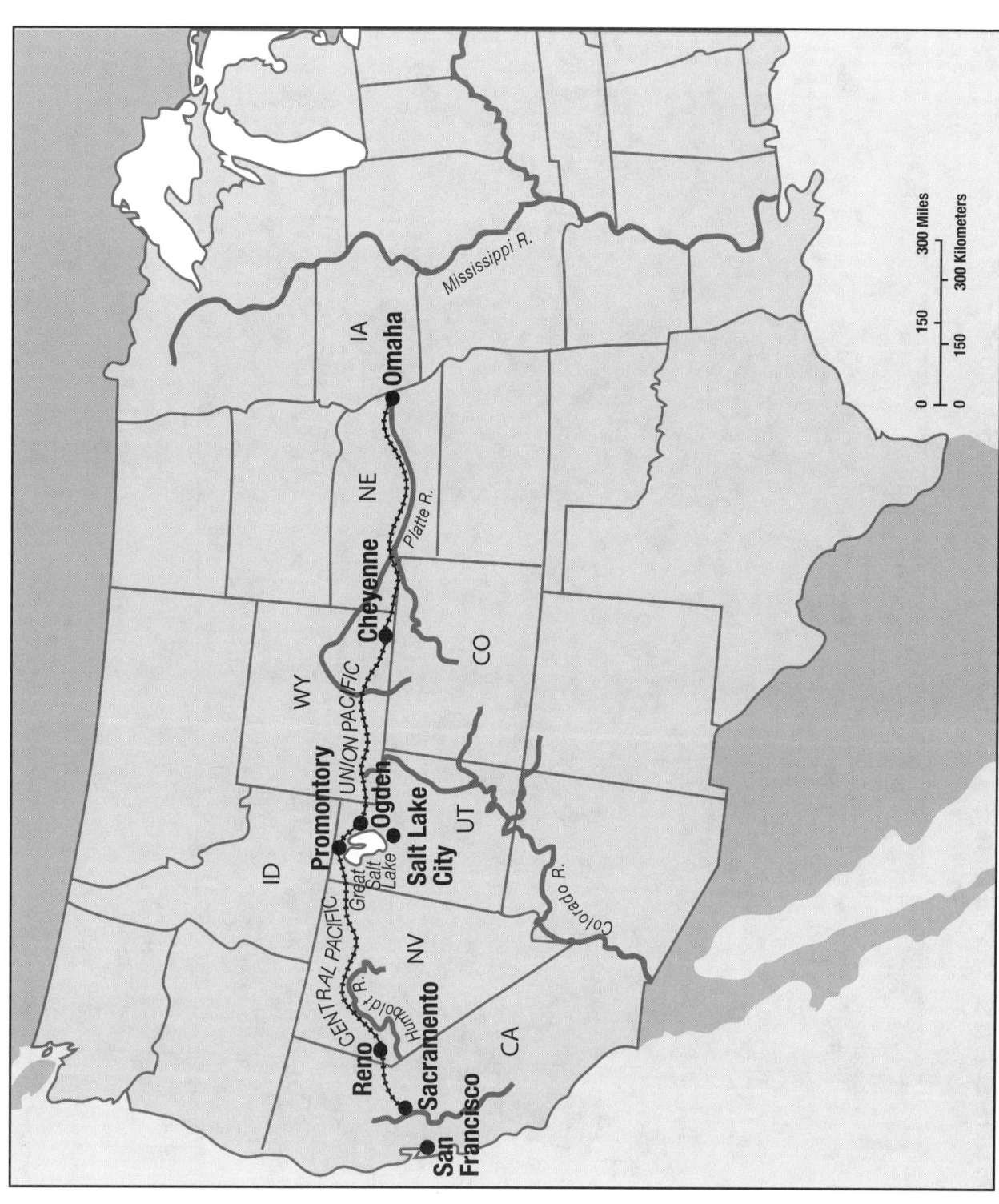

Name: _____   Date: _____

Railroads and Growth in the West, 1890

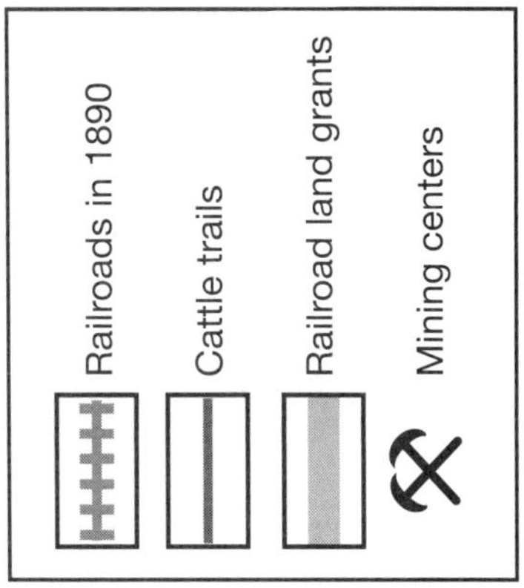

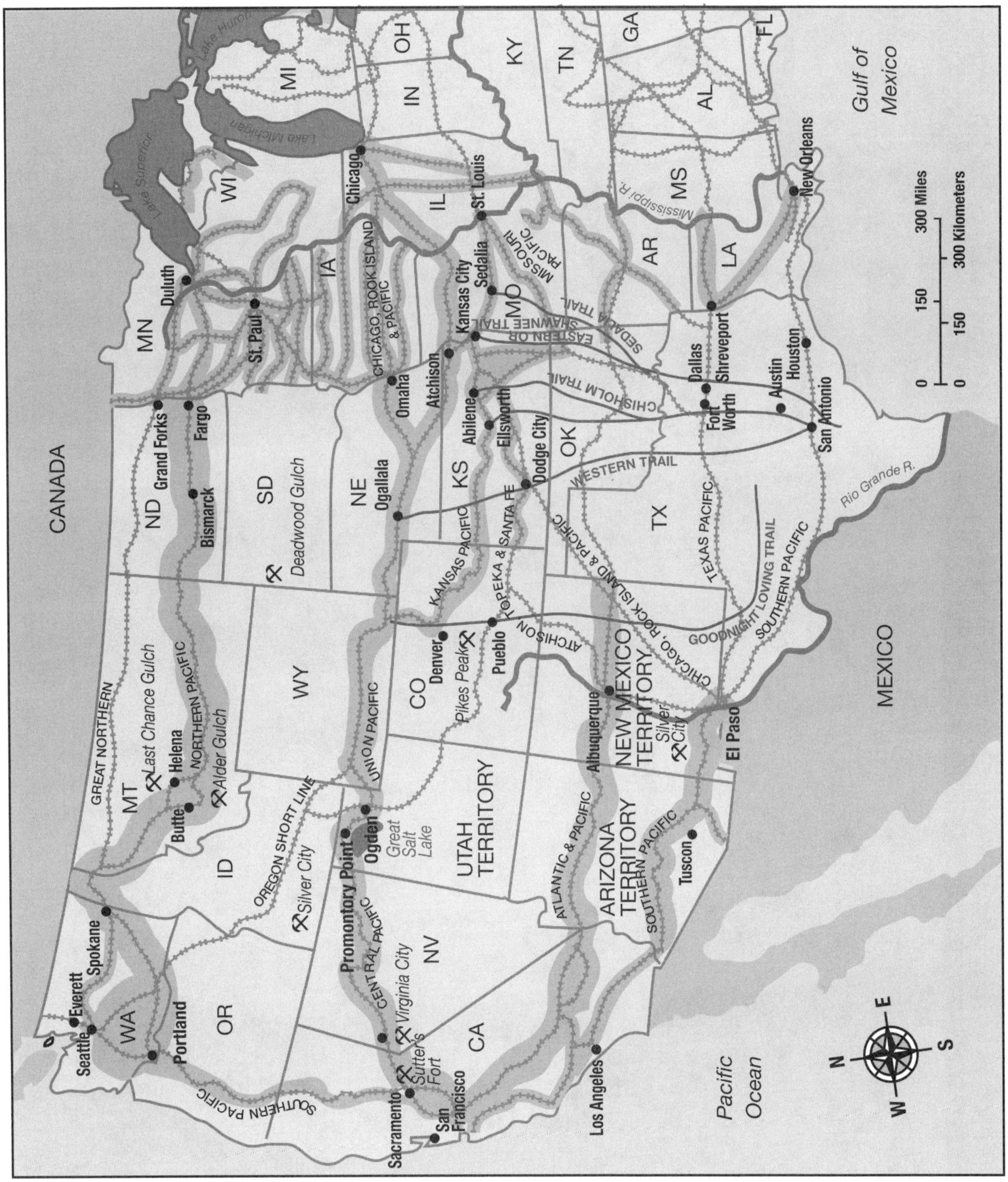

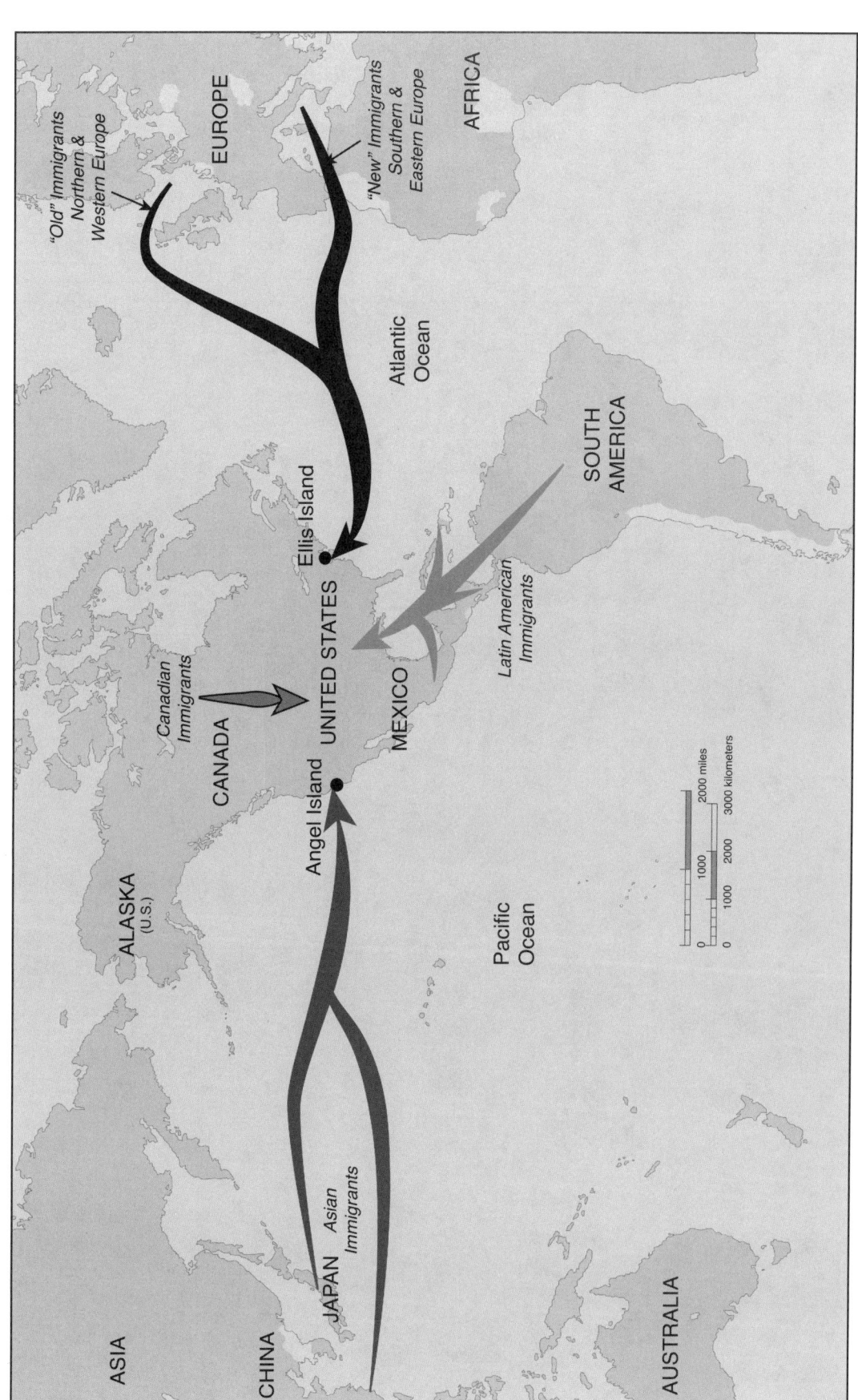

Maps for U.S. History

Routes of the Klondike Gold Rush

Name: _____ Date: _____

Routes of the Klondike Gold Rush

Map #: 073

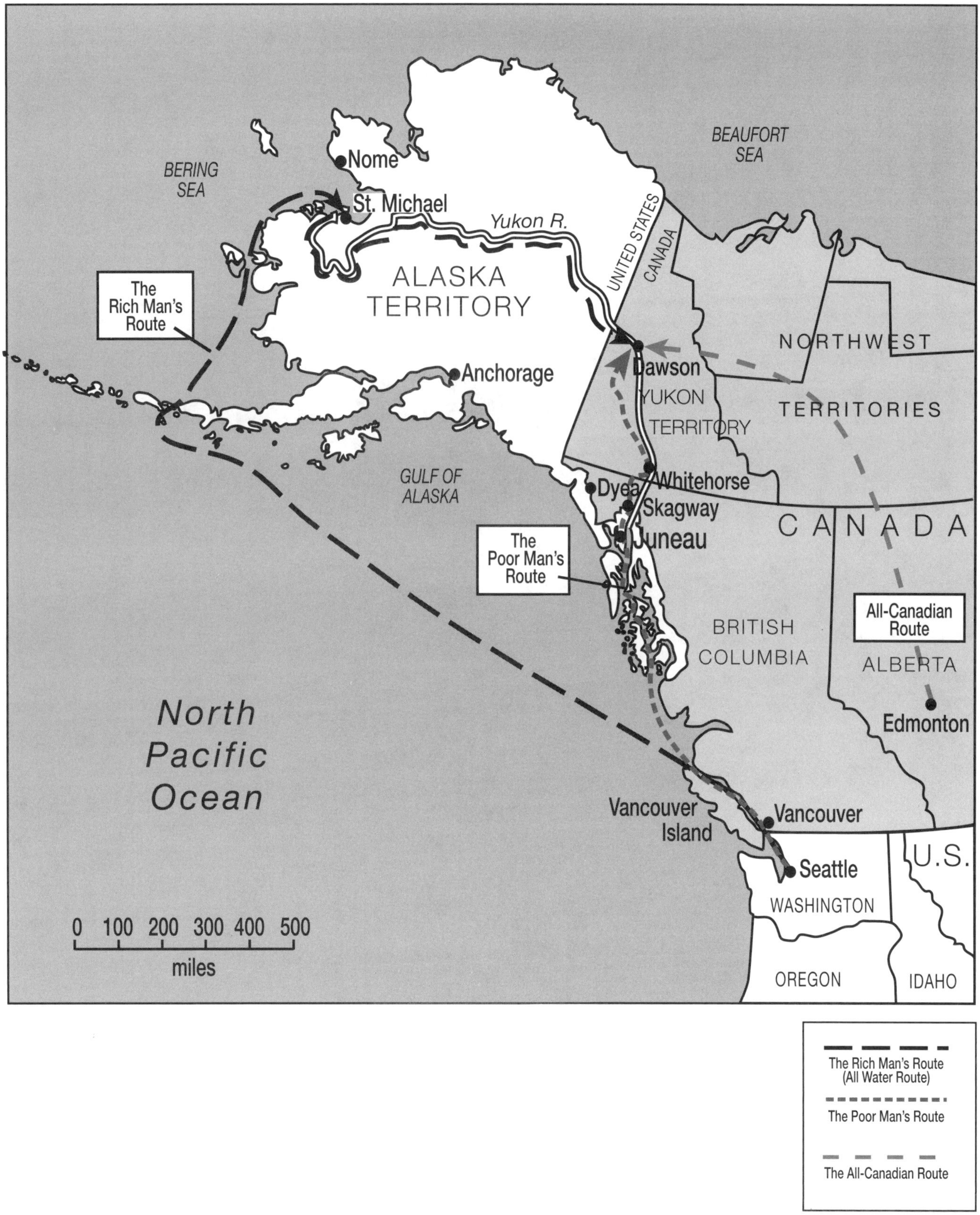

Name: _____ Date: _____

Spanish-American War

Maps for U.S. History — Spanish-American War

Map #: 074

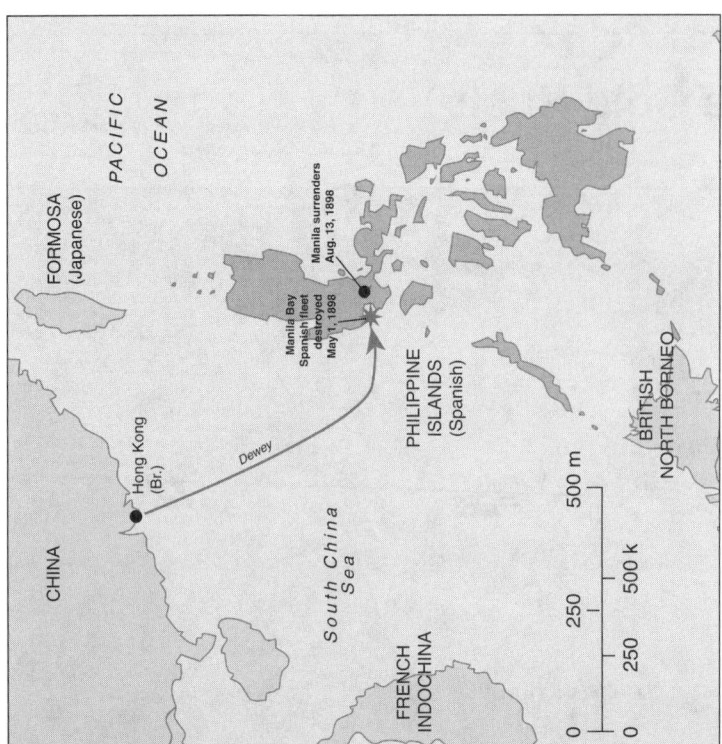

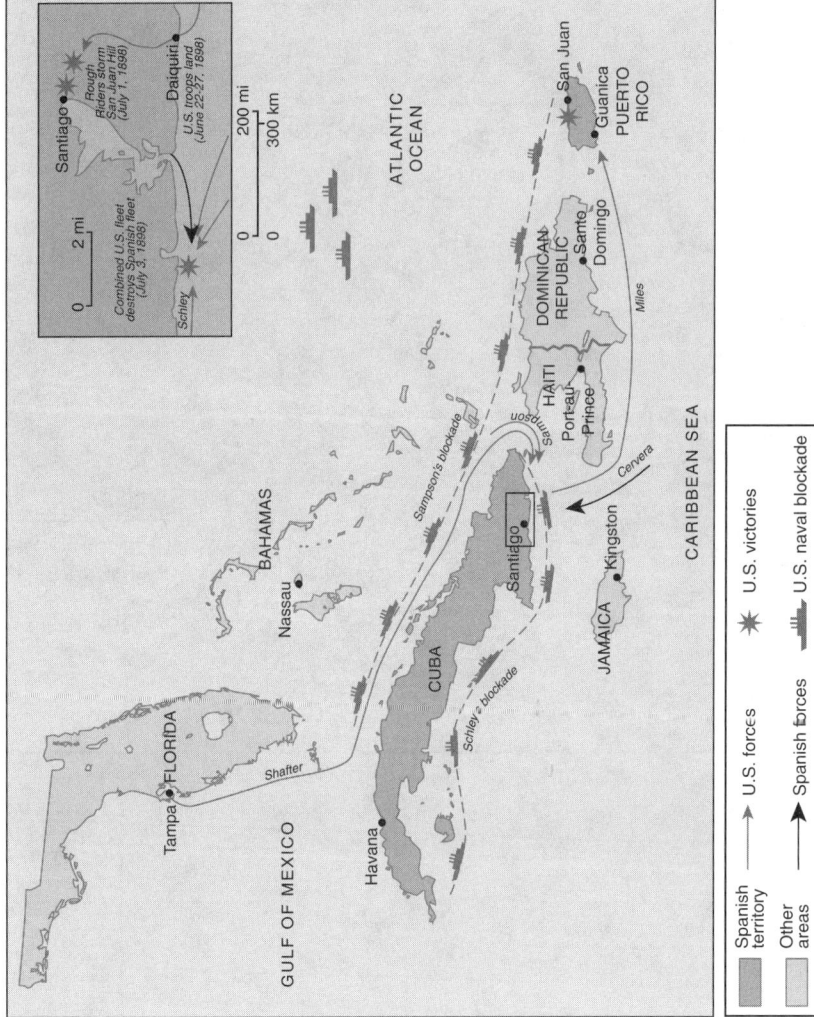

Maps for U.S. History

Dust Bowl, 1930s

Name: _____

Date: _____

Dust Bowl, 1930s

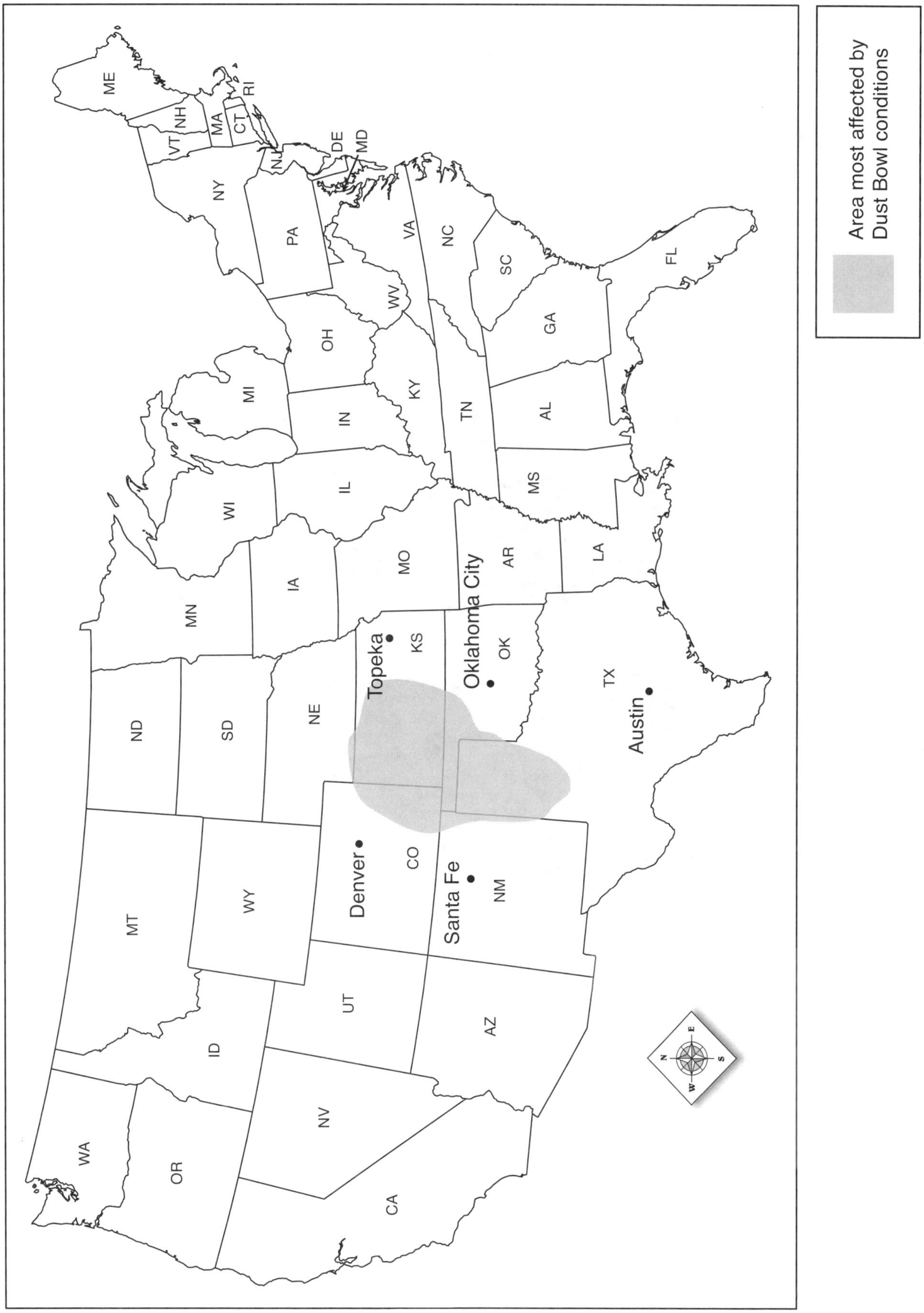

Map #: 075

Area most affected by Dust Bowl conditions

Name: _____ Date: _____

Climate Regions of the United States

Maps for U.S. History

Map #: 076

Climate Regions of the United States

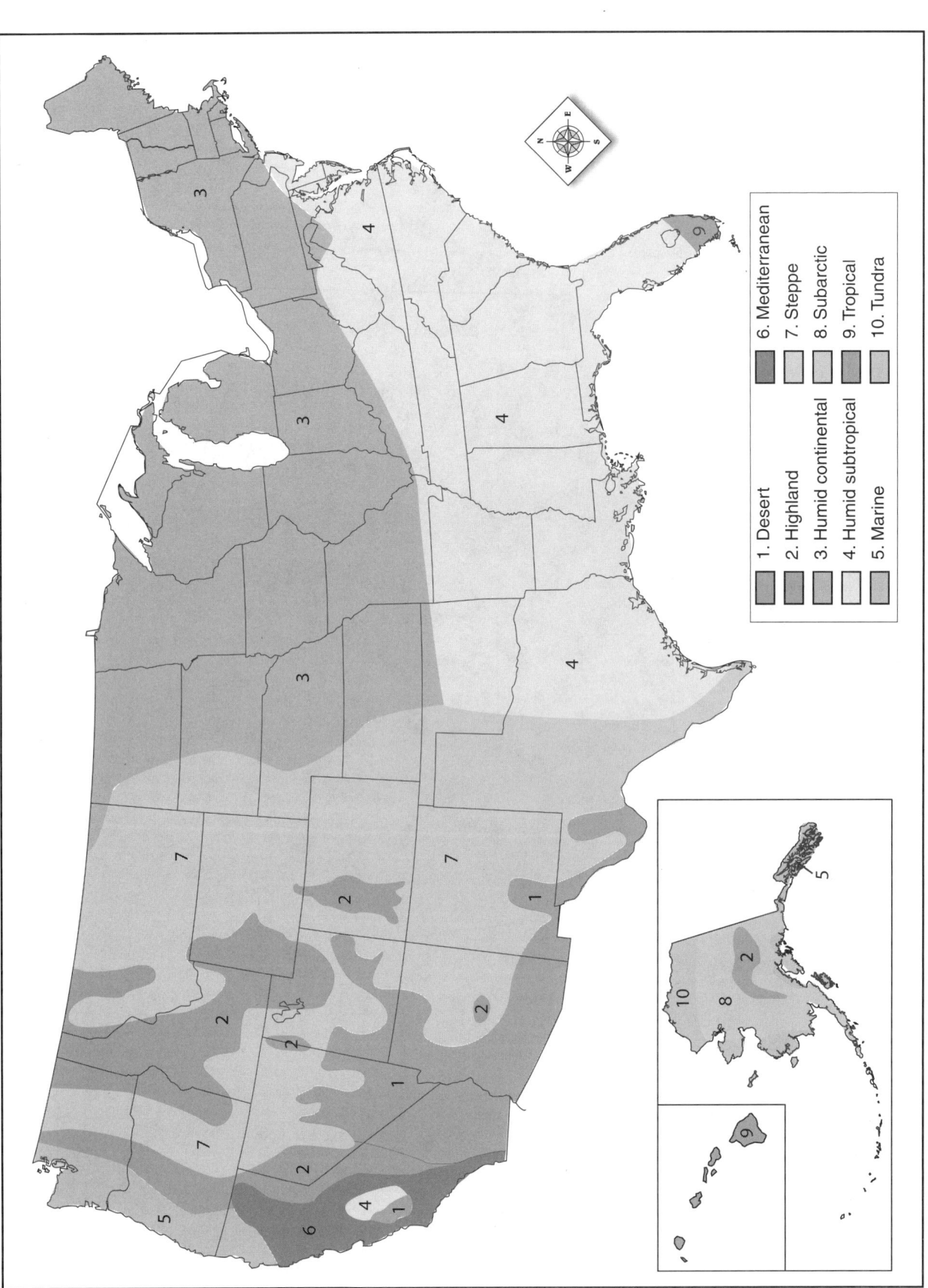